Exploring strategic financial management

Tony Grundy
with Gerry Johnson & Kevan Scholes

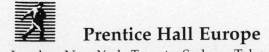

Prentice Hall Europe

London New York Toronto Sydney Tokyo Singapore
Madrid Mexico City Munich Paris

First published 1998 by
Prentice Hall Europe
Campus 400, Maylands Avenue
Hemel Hempstead
Hertfordshire, HP2 7EZ
A division of Simon & Schuster International Group

Typeset in 10/12 pt New Century Schoolbook with Meta
by Hart McLeod, Cambridge

Printed and bound in Great Britain
by T.J. International Ltd, Cornwall

Library of Congress Cataloging in Publication Data
Grundy, Tony, 1954–
Exploring strategic financial management / Tony Grundy, with Gerry
Johnson & Kevan Scholes.
    p.   cm.
Includes bibliographical references and index.
ISBN 0-13-570102-3
1. Corporations – Finance. 2. Strategic planning.
I. Johnson, Gerry. II. Scholes, Kevan, III Title.
HG4026.G87 1998
658. 15–dc21
97–38466 CIP

British Library Cataloguing in Publication Data
A catalogue record for this book is available from
the British Library

ISBN 0–13–570102–3

1 2 3 4 5 02 01 00 99 98

Contents

Figures

Tables

Illustrations

Case studies

Preface

Exploring Corporate Strategy by Gerry Johnson and Kevan Scholes is now established as the leading text in its field in Europe and beyond with world-wide sales exceeding 300,000. It is a text for students and practising managers which aims to develop their conceptual understanding of why and how organisations of many different types develop and change their strategies. It does so within a practical context whilst drawing on the best strategic management practice as researchers, writers and practitioners understand it.

With so many managers and students now familiar with *Exploring Corporate Strategy,* we have responded to the requests for material which takes the themes and concepts of strategic management further, in a way which is not possible within the confines of a broad textbook on the subject. Prentice Hall Europe is publishing a series of short, practical books which build on the basic framework of *Exploring Corporate Strategy*. This book on Exploring Strategic Financial Management is one of the first two books to be published in the series. the other is *Techniques of Analysis and Evaluation of Strategic Management* by Veronique Ambrosini. These books are developed under the editorial guidance of Gerry Johnson and Kevan Scholes and have the following aims:

- to provide further depth on aspects of strategic management which should already be familiar to readers of *Exploring Corporate Strategy.*
- to do this in a practical and applied way whilst drawing on best practice from researchers, writers and practitioners.

At first sight, corporate strategy and financial management may not seem to be easy bed-fellows. In reconciling both disciplines, one is reminded of a children's favourite story-book which has two monsters – one blue and one red. As the sun goes down one monster says,

'Day is ending'

whilst the other monster says

'Night is beginning'.

The two monsters begin a furious argument, hurling stones at each other until they collapse exhausted. Eventually, they realise that they are both in agreement (having used up an entire mountain in their pointless battle).

Corporate strategy and financial management seem to bear an uncanny resemblance to our blue and red monsters. Corporate strategy focuses on the ambiguous, the uncertain, the less tangible and qualitative, whilst financial management emphasises the precise, the measurable, and the tangible. But out of the rubble of existing management theories we are now seeing a new discipline emerge, that of: STRATEGIC FINANCIAL MANAGEMENT.

Strategic financial management can be defined as:

'The assessment of strategic options, choices and business performance by both strategic *and* financial analysis.'

Strategic financial management thus enables managers to overcome the great divide between strategic and financial analysis prevailing in many companies. So acute can this divide become that it can result in corporate schizophrenia. This schizophrenia can become so ingrained that it is hardly even noticeable. Managers may not even be aware that they espouse a strategic vision which cuts completely across financial potential and constraints. Equally, they may not be aware that the financial projections used to target action are fundamentally incompatible with business and competitive realities.

Exploring Strategic Financial Management examines how a united view of strategic and financial issues can become a practical reality. This is achieved by looking at:

- the links between corporate strategy and strategic financial management
- managing for value – enabling financial management to play a positive and proactive role in strategic management
- the processes of value management – these include strategic management accounting, strategic financial accounting and strategic and financial planning
- key applications, including strategic investment decisions, acquisitions, strategic cost management and valuing business change
- implementing strategic financial management.

The book is structured as a practical guide with plenty of checklists and case examples. Although it is of obvious appeal to MBA students and undergraduates, it is of equal relevance to practising managers, whether these hold financial or non-financial roles. The Chief Executive, Finance Director and other senior executives should feel comfortable reading it, and relaxed to be seen using it on an everyday basis.

Tony Grundy
Gerry Johnson
Kevan Scholes 1997

Acknowledgements

I am greatly indebted to Kevan Scholes, Editor and Co-Author of *Exploring Corporate Strategy*, who provided me with an anchor for my ideas throughout and without whose help this book would not have been written.

I would also like to thank Pat Edwards who once again coped with my changing ideas stream with her usual calm.

Particular thanks go to David Shephard (formerly of IDV), Karen Slatford (Hewlett Packard), Catherine Steer (re Tesco supermarket trolleys – the cost drivers) and Simon Hart, Head of Corporate Planning at Rolls-Royce Aeroengines. I also thank Sophie Castell, Kath Taylor and Julie Watson (former MBA students) for their research on the football industry, giving them the recognition which they deserve.

Final word

I would also invite any manager who wishes to discuss strategic financial management issues with me to contact me at Cranfield (tel: 01234 751122).

Tony Grundy, 1997

Part 1
Introduction

Chapter 1 lays out our task – of integrating corporate strategy much more closely with financial management. Both strategy and finance can be seen as 'dry' subjects – but we will show not only how they are very practical, but also how they go hand in hand.

Finance, itself, is not simply a technical discipline but is actually interesting, challenging and potentially very stretching and creative – if deployed in the right way. Equally, strategy can and must be steered in the direction of adding shareholder value.

When strategy and finance work closely together (as strategic financial management), many of the behavioural difficulties of managing short- versus long-term, or external versus internal, priorities, become much reduced.

1 Introducing strategic financial management

1.1 Introduction

Throughout *Exploring Corporate Strategy* there are very many references to financial analysis. Our job is to develop these references *and to integrate corporate strategy much more closely into financial management*.

At first sight we have a tough challenge ahead. For both strategy and finance can be seen as 'dry' and often difficult subjects by many managers. Both disciplines have been at least partly guilty in the past of appearing to be esoteric, technical and distanced from everyday management practice. *Exploring Corporate Strategy* by Gerry Johnson and Kevan Scholes is aimed at making strategic management more accessible. We continue this tradition by making the border between strategy and finance – Strategic Financial Management – equally accessible.

Just as strategy teaches us to turn threats into opportunities, we therefore begin by putting you more at ease with our two disciplines. Let us take finance first. With the exception of hardened accountants, the very word 'finance' can induce a trance-like state, somewhat akin to fear in many of us.

So, let us begin by asking: what the letters F I N A N C E really stand for? In our view they mean:

F   for Fun
I   for Interesting
N   for Nasty (when things go wrong)
A   for Advantage (personally – to your career)
N   for *not* precise
C   for Creative
E   for Exciting.

Fun: to begin with finance is, contrary to many managers' expectations, *fun*. Once you have overcome the initial off-putting technical terms, it becomes enjoyable to tease out the financial implications of strategic thinking, or to see through a smokescreen surrounding many companies' published accounts.

Interesting: finance is interesting: but only if you are prepared to make the linkages with the business environment, with competitive position, and across business processes and functions. (This is not to say that finance is not at times a serious business, merely that the application of financial techniques can be inherently enjoyable, as many managers have found.)

Nasty: finance can of course turn *nasty* if it is mismanaged. In Europe, and particularly in the UK, investors have had their fair share of corporate and financial disasters over the last ten years. Hopefully these can be avoided in future. Financial failure is frequently the result of strategic drift or misguided strategic decisions.

Advantage: finance can also help to give you (personally) advantage in your career. Many managers never really feel at ease with finance, let alone in how it links to strategy. They run a very real risk of becoming the hostages of their accountants.

Precision: finance is certainly *not* precise. If you are looking for exact measurement in finance then you will inevitably be disappointed. Precise financial management can actually be highly misleading. *Invariably, any financial plan or statement is supported by a hidden fabric of judgements, assumptions and interpretations.* You should always remember the GIGO rule of Garbage-In and Garbage-Out.

Creative: because financial management is imprecise it is often a *creative* discipline too. This creativity can be either positive or harmful, depending upon how it is applied.

Exciting: finally, finance is certainly a potentially *exciting* discipline. It is often through the financial lens that the ambiguity of strategy can at least be partially resolved. Financial thinking can stretch strategic vision – for example by asking the question 'what would we have to achieve strategically to secure a particular financial result?'.

Finance is thus given an essential and helpful framework for guiding strategic management *provided that it is not misapplied or misunderstood*. If finance now seems to be a little more manager-friendly, we are now faced with a similar task in demystifying strategy. Although strategy is seen by business school professors and at least by some MBA students as quite exciting, many practising managers view it as distant, mysterious and even cloaked in secrecy and danger. In our view, strategy is a most practical, everyday tool. The letters in 'strategy' should stand for:

S for Simplicity
T for Thinking
R for a Results-focus
A for Action
T for Timing
E for Energising
G for Goal-driven
Y for Your future.

Simplicity: to begin with the most successful strategies exemplify *simplicity*. Simplicity resides in their being a relatively few number of competitive fundamentals which are lined up to deliver value. For instance, at the bank First Direct in the UK, simplicity resides in brand differentiation, service excellence and first-mover advantage. At the supermarket chain Tesco, in the UK, this depends upon a brand identity based on convenience, friendly service and value for money. Whilst First Direct has a tightly focused market strategy, Tesco's is broad. But both companies share 'simplicity' in their core business.

Simplicity is directly targeted at achieving maximum potential value out of the strategy. For example, both First Direct and Tesco aim to create high market share (or niche share) and very strong customer loyalty which feeds back into reasonable margins, a steady and natural flow of new customers, and a platform for further strategic development.

Thinking: strategy is also about *thinking*, which does not necessarily occur easily in the pressure of everyday management. Strategy involves reflecting on where you are now, exploring where you want to be, and how to get there. (This should be underpinned by thinking in parallel, and not afterwards, about what this means in terms of value generation and investment.)

Results-focus: strategy is also about *results*. Strategy can look superb on paper but prove wanting in delivering market, operational and financial results. Strategies do not necessarily have very easily quantified value. Strategies are, in effect, like gambling chips – they are of interest in that they can generate financial return. But at any point in time their future return is imprecise, as it is contingent on future events.

But these same strategies ultimately have value only if and when they are cashed in for real money. (It would be a very strange strategy game if one had to wait forever to see if one could get some financial return.) Strategy un-truth number one is 'If something is labelled "strategic" it means we don't have to deliver any specific results'.

Action: strategy must also therefore be about *action*. One of the common failings of strategic plans is that assumed follow-through action simply does not happen. According to the (former) Director of Strategic Planning, BP Belgium:

> 'In the past many of our (strategic plans) suffered droop – in fact we now call this phenomenon "strategic droop", and we hold up all our new business plans against the "strategic droop test".'

To illustrate 'strategic droop', consider Figure 1.1. Here profit projections in the business planning cycle always appear to be over-optimistic, but each year the bias to optimism re-occurs.

The phenomenon of strategic droop might be caused by a variety of factors. For instance, it may be due to weak strategic analysis. Or the strategic analysis may have been done well but the financial realities of the strategy may not have been well defined. Or, because managers are not held accountable for *both* the strategic and financial performance of the business, they can continue to misjudge the future and get away with it.

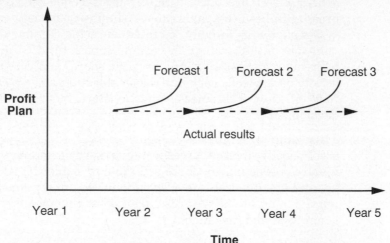

Figure 1.1   Business planning and financial drift

Timing: following on from strategic droop, we might also have a similar droop in financial performance. Strategy very much requires close attention to the *timing*, specifically of external events or other competitive conditions. Many strategies might well yield value provided that they are launched either *before* a particular time or *no later than* another time. This 'time-window' of a strategy can have a profound impact on its financial value. For example, Bill Gates of Microsoft (1) suggested that IBM forfeited leadership in the emergent sector of the information technology industry in the 1980s because it simply did not respond quickly enough to fundamentally new competitive conditions. Yet timing is often a neglected issue in many strategy and financial management texts.

Energising: strategy is, potentially an *energising* force. A key way in which strategy adds value is by providing fresh vigour and sense of purpose into managers otherwise buffeted by operational turbulence. But this energy must be controlled very carefully otherwise financial value will be diluted or destroyed, for example through ill-advised business expansion or diversification. Here, financial discipline should not be seen as the unalterable constraint on a particular strategy but as a prompt to generate more appropriate options to fulfil both strategic and financial goals, which we turn to next.

Goal-driven: strategy means clear linkages with specific operational and financial *goals*. This means not just setting direction, but also establishing controls (strategic and financial). Planning and control can be mistakenly taken as virtually separate processes. But to be truly effective, a relatively seamless interface between planning and control processes needs to be woven. This means that the key business controls and measures must be considered *during* strategy formulation (both in analysis and choice – see *Exploring Corporate Strategy*), and not afterwards.

Future: finally, strategy is about *your future*. Although many managers may *say* they have a strategy, what proportion actually use strategy as the hub of their management process? (Managers often seem to see strategy as more of ornamental significance than as a real management tool. It is something they have been told they must have some time in their careers, without being told what its practical benefit actually is.) By integrating strategy more closely with finance we are able to show how strategy is relevant, because the question is now always asked 'what is the value (financially) of the strategy?'

Both finance and strategy are very closely linked in the role they should play in the management process. This is no accident, for both strategy and finance have (in part) common antecedents, particularly as both have strong roots in economic theory.

Competitive strategy has close linkages with industrial (or 'micro') economics, whilst finance is derived, to a great extent, from financial economics. (A second influence – accountancy – is also at work in financial management. Unfortunately the application of accountancy techniques has perhaps put too much emphasis on past, current and future short-term performance.)

But for a long time the two disciplines of strategy and financial management have run on separate tracks both in the academic world and in the world of business. However, we now have the possibility of re-coupling them on the main line of *strategic financial management*. In the remainder of our introduction we now examine the key links between corporate strategy and financial analysis, dealing particularly with:

- strategic analysis
- strategic choice
- strategy implementation
- strategy, value and learning.

1.2   *Strategic analysis*

In strategic analysis we need to analyse our current strategic capability, the expectations of our stakeholders and our culture, and the business environment. In *Exploring Corporate Strategy* (Section 1.2.1) a number of levels of analysis are listed. In Table 1.1 we now present the linkages between strategic and financial analysis.

Examining Table 1.1 more closely, there does not seem to be a major mismatch in the focus of both sets of analysis between strategy and finance. Indeed, if it were not for a third influence – management behaviour (culture and politics), as discussed extensively in *Exploring Corporate Strategy* – there might be a more ready convergence in practice between the twin disciplines. (We see these tensions very much to the fore in the case study of a major plc in our concluding Chapter 8.)

Table 1.1   *Strategic analysis and financial analysis*

	Strategic analysis	Financial analysis
Mission	• Is it stretching but achievable?	• Does this mission guide (or misguide) strategy development?
	• And is it the essence of what we are about?	• Does it distract or even destroy shareholder value?
Objectives	• What are our strategic goals?	• Are these consistent with financial realities? Present and future?
Strategies	• How do we achieve our goals – with competitive advantage?	• What is the value of these strategies?
Actions	• Do these support our strategies?	• What is the value of the sets of strategic decisions ('strategic project set')?
	• Are these sufficient?	
Control	• What strategic milestones do we need to pass, and when?	• What financial returns (profit and cash) do we expect?

Whilst the world of both (deliberate) strategic management and financial theory are rational, prescriptive and almost a-human, the business reality is very different. Business managers face the continual challenge of making day-to-day trade-offs with both strategic and financial impact based on imperfect data and with too little time to think. They also have to cope with the interplay between politics (because of conflicting expectations of stakeholders), personalities and even prejudice. Whilst we cannot ignore this behavioural turbulence, without the *structuring influence* of strategy and finance we might find it impossible to manage complex businesses. That is not to say that management behaviour, culture and politics are *not* central – indeed they are, but that strategy and finance can help to *channel* some of the more volatile management dilemmas and debates so that some decisions are actually possible.

1.3 *Strategic choice*

Following our comparison of strategic and financial analysis, we now link strategic choice with financial evaluation (whilst also addressing some of the behavioural issues). Returning once more to the core concepts of *Exploring Corporate Strategy* (see Section 8.1), Table 1.2 once again highlights the close fit between strategy and finance.

Table 1.2 Examining strategic options

	Strategic choice	Financial evaluation	Behavioural influences
Suitability	• What are the competitive benefits (now and future)? • What entry barriers and switching costs can be created and how can our lead be maintained?	• What are the benefits/costs of exploiting it? • What will it cost to develop and protect this position?	• Do we really want to work this hard? • How do we reinforce commitment to make it happen?
Acceptability	• Is this acceptable to *all* stakeholders?	• Is the level of returns consistent with risk?	• What are stakeholders' agendas and how can we steer these?
Feasibility	• Is there a market opportunity and have we the capability?	• Is the opportunity within our financial constraints?	• Do we really believe it is possible?

Suitability first of all covers the fit between its competitive environment and the organisation's competence. This can be measured through the competitive benefits from the strategy, either by protecting or enhancing current position, and also through building future position. But equally we need to evaluate the financial benefits and costs of exploiting any strategic options. Managers may also need to address whether they really want to work this hard to achieve success.

Suitability also focuses, for instance, on making it hard for others to copy or imitate a successful competitive strategy (this is frequently described as the 'sustainability' of the strategy). This might involve, for example, investing in barriers to entry, in building switching costs of customers (or suppliers). (Switching costs are the perceived or real costs of changing to another supplier, for example the search costs, learning costs and the perceived risk of switching.) Or it may mean testing out how (and precisely how) an assumed competitive lead can be sustained. But, equally, this needs to be married to *how much it will cost* to develop and then protect this competitive position.

Equally, we must not neglect the behavioural processes needed to reinforce commitment of staff throughout the organisation. These processes will include annual reviews of performance, increasingly continued tenure in job, and hopefully career progression and bonus payments. Strategic financial management most certainly *does not* end with performance measurement – it needs to feed its influence into corporate rewards and recognition, and directly.

Acceptability in strategic choice entails taking the perspective of a variety of key stakeholders. Do they find this particular strategic choice one with which they are comfortable? Or, if they are uncomfortable, to what extent can they live with it? If it is very uncomfortable, is their mind-set one of 'despite the pain this is an area which we must simply make some tough decisions on'? This leads ultimately into uncovering stakeholder agendas and actually proactively seeking to re-align these with strategic vision (and aspirations for creating financial value).

Acceptability also involves thinking through whether the level of financial returns is consistent with the level of risk. Here we are not merely looking at a shareholder perspective but also at whether managers themselves are comfortable with the existing balance of return and risk. When managers inadvertently destroy shareholder value through making inappropriate strategic decisions they also – in the same breath – destroy future jobs in their organisation, and undermine their own career prospects. Only the very fast movers in management (and a few do exist) are likely to escape in the long term the adverse consequences of poor strategic (and financial) decisions.

Feasibility for instance concerns whether there is both an external market opportunity worthwhile addressing – and also the capability within the organisation to address it effectively. This includes identifying whether it is compatible with financial constraints (in terms of the investment requirement, and cash flow). Besides the strategic and financial evaluation management need to reflect on whether they actually believe the strategy is actually possible.

1.4 *Strategy implementation*

Exploring Corporate Strategy emphasises the importance of implementation in strategic management. Implementation is all too often the 'graveyard of strategy', and one of the contributory causes of this is weak linkage between strategic and financial thinking and analysis.

Table 1.3 once again illustrates the key links between strategic and financial analysis. The vision for organisational change needs probing in terms of its strategic rationale, and in terms of its finance impact (based on before-and-after analysis of the change). Also, the analysis is incomplete without examining behavioural issues such as perceived implications of the strategic vision. These behavioural issues also require examining how happy or unhappy staff are with the status quo – and their potential fear of major change. Remember that the value of a strategic change programme could be uncontested in strategic and financial terms, but realising its value could be frustrated simply through organisational inertia.

Table 1.3   Strategy implementation

	Strategic analysis	Financial analysis	Behavioural issues
Organisational structure and design	What organisational structures will meet the competitive challenge?	What value is added, diluted or destroyed by a specific organisational structure?	Will a particular structure add value given our culture?
Resource allocation and control	What businesses should we invest more in or less in and what competitive performance do we expect?	What is the likely impact of resource decisions on financial performance?	What will prevent us from re-allocating resource to where it needs to go?
Managing change	What key changes are needed to support the strategy and how should these be managed?	What is the targeted value of organisational change programmes (and their cost)?	What behaviours would either enhance or erode the value of organisational change?

'Strategic choice' is normally associated with the phase prior to strategy implementation (because it is focused on external, competitive positioning). But during the initial phase of implementation there may be a *second phase* of strategic choice: the selection of the specific programmes and priorities which will actually provide the vehicles for implementation. Finance can assist us here by helping put some (approximate) value on the change.

Strategic change programmes fall into two categories: *Transformational change* and *Continuous improvement*. Illustration 1.1 gives some examples of transformational change for a multinational computer company.

Strategy in action

illustration 1.1

Implementation and value in a multinational computer company

Transformational change may seem an abstract notion, but when we examine specific transformational change programmes these do have some very specific financial benefits which can be quantified.

Transformational change	Key financial benefits
• Product simplification.	• Reduced product costs.
• Business process re-engineering.	• Reduced processes costs.
• Acquisitions and alliances.	• More revenues, margins and future opportunities.
• Organisational flexibility.	• Accelerates product launches – more revenues and margins.

Continuous improvement	Key financial benefits
• Quality management.	• Avoids loss of customers and lost revenues – and reduces costs.
• Out-sourcing non-core activities.	• Improves margins and reduces costs of distraction.
• Management skills.	• Costly management errors avoided. New opportunities created and harvested.
• Team building.	• Costs of undue political activity avoided.

Note that in some cases the key financial benefits are more tangible and easily measured than in others. For instance, product simplification may give rise to easy-to-measure cost reduction, whilst quality management may reduce the risks of loss of customers – but we would need to isolate the occasions here where customers were lost *principally as a result of poor quality*. We explore the issue of dealing with intangibles further in Chapter 5 on 'Strategic Investment Decisions'.

1.5   *Strategy, value and learning*

To summarise, Figure 1.2 now develops the Analysis – Choice – Implementation framework in *Exploring Corporate Strategy* to embrace financial analysis.

This highlights that out of the *analysis* phase we see the first cut *valuation* of competitive strategies. This is an overall assessment of whether these competitive strategies are likely to add to, dilute, or even destroy shareholder value. Not only does this require a *financial* assessment of existing and potential future competitive position, but also a scenario (or picture of the future) of the business environment.

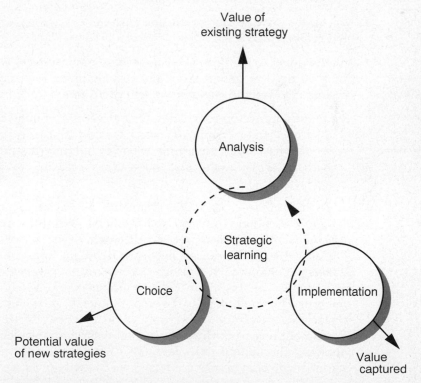

Figure 1.2   *Strategic management, learning and value*

This scenario should embrace both a number of competitive and financial assumptions.

In the centre of the three Analysis – Choice – Implementation circles we also highlight the process of *strategic learning*. (See Figure 1.2.)

In common with other strategic management processes, one of the most valuable outputs from strategic financial management is strategic learning. Strategic learning occurs when managers reflect on their strategic *and financial recipes* which consciously – or unconsciously – drive the decision-making process. This may result in insights, including:

- our views on 'what businesses we are in' or 'should be in' need to change. For instance, by probing a business area *both* strategically *and* financially, managers may come to the conclusion that there are bleak prospects for achieving real competitive advantage and adequate financial returns

- whether we can (or cannot) make sufficient financial returns out of certain kinds of business. For instance, managers might decide that certain types of business have levels of margins which are just *too low* to sustain business and corporate overhead levels – which are aimed at supporting more complex business

- we need to review our profit and cash-generation expectations, or our investment priorities

- due to adverse shifts in the competitive environment we must realise that we need to undertake major restructuring and reductions in our cost base to remain competitive and profitable

- we may come to the conclusion that sales in our existing business are likely to become a commodity purchase and that to survive we need to seek out new and emerging ways of adding distinctive value to customers. This might also necessitate creating or acquiring new competencies.

To summarise, strategic financial management enables us to integrate strategic thinking and financial planning, and analysis and control as an integrated process. Although, as we see in Table 1.4, there are some key differences between strategic analysis and financial analysis, these are not so large that we cannot integrate the two.

Financial analysis can also be linked very closely with external analysis, for instance by tracing financial variables back to their underlying (and often external) value drivers. Further, there is no fundamental reason why financial analysis cannot be long term; indeed applying discounted cash flow (DCF) financial analysis is the most natural way of evaluating a longer-term strategy as we will see in our conclusion in the case study of 'TDC plc'.

Table 1.4   *Contrasting strategic and financial analysis*

Strategic analysis...	Financial analysis...
captures a wide range of variables – both external and internal	focuses on a narrower range of variables – primarily internal
evaluates tangible and less tangible areas of value	is primarily concerned with tangible areas of value
involves mainly qualitative measures	involves more quantitative measures
has longer-term horizons	has a bias towards shorter-term (with some exceptions)
is about creative thinking	is more about the control process
deals with broader uncertainties	employs techniques for measuring specific risks.

1.6 *Structure of the book*

In Part 2 we see that value analysis can be focused either towards the *future* – through strategic management accounting or towards the *past* – through strategic financial accounting. Figure 1.3 overleaf lays out the structure of our book.

Chapter 1 (which forms Part 1) has introduced the book which is now concerned with two main themes.

Firstly, the tools and techniques of Value Analysis which are explored in Chapters 2, 3 and 4.

Chapters 5, 6 and 7 (which form Part 3) deal with strategic and financial development both internally (investment in Chapter 5, cost management in Chapter 7), and externally (acquisitions in Chapter 6).

Finally, Chapter 8 (which forms Part 4 – Implementing Strategic Financial Management) reviews the key themes and lessons from the book, and focuses on some key implementation issues, addressing these in a case study on SFM process at a major plc.

In our book, short case studies are shown as Illustrations in the text, but where we have large case studies these are contained in the main body of the book, to maintain the flow.

1.7 *Key questions*

Before you turn to Chapter 2, please spend a few minutes reflecting on the following two key questions:

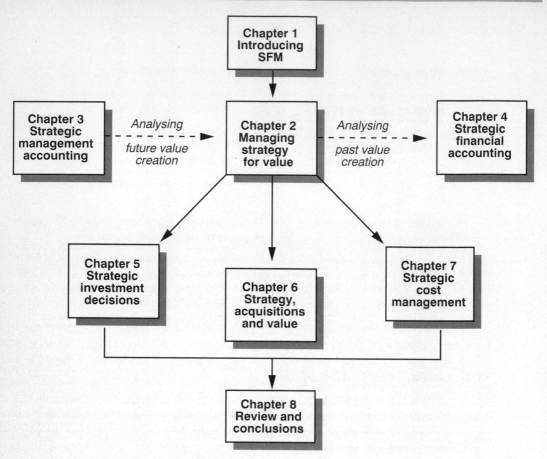

Figure 1.3   The structure of our book

- is 'finance' seen as primarily a policing operation in your organisation? How has financial analysis added value in the past by helping change the way you looked at strategic options? What future opportunities for using financial analysis for *creative advantage* can you identify?
- are you able to integrate strategic and financial thinking easily in management debate, or does your team exhibit mild or acute finance-stratophrenia? How can you begin to break down the barriers in mind-set, perhaps by getting financially-led thinkers to be deliberately visionary, and strategy-led thinkers to focus critically on value-added?

References

(1) Gates B, *The Road Ahead*, Viking, 1995

Part 2
Value analysis

In Part 2 we explore how value is created, how it can be analysed and then managed in a variety of organisations.

Chapter 2 on 'Managing Strategy for Value' takes us deeper into how value is created in business. We examine value and cost drivers – both within the competitive and in the internal environment. We then consider the importance of the fact that finance has a cost (the cost of capital) dependent upon how the financial markets perceive a Group.

Chapter 2 also helps us to relate specifically the strategic analysis tools of *Exploring Corporate Strategy* with their financial implications. We then turn to the basis of value creation – and address the questions 'What is the business value system, how does it operate, and how can it be managed?' Finally, we illustrate the business value system, and how it can migrate over time (either deliberately or in an emergent fashion) by examining Manchester United and the Association Football industry.

Chapter 3 then helps us to understand how financial and strategic performance (both present and future) can be linked. In Strategic Management Accounting we bring together life-cycle effects, product/market positioning and operations management in managing strategic and financial performance. Strategic Management Accounting is then illustrated by the Virgin Financial Industry case study.

Finally, in Chapter 4 ('Strategic Financial Accounting') we show how useful past analysis of a company's financial performance can give us important clues and insights into future financial *and* strategic performance.

2 *Managing strategy for value*

2.1 *Introduction*

In our second chapter we explore in more depth how competitive strategy can be valued. This begins by a high-level examination of the existing theories on corporate strategy and shareholder value. This covers the idea that a financial value can be put on a business strategy, and that this is achieved by generating a return higher than the cost of capital. This superior return requires the management of specific value and cost drivers (and critical success factors). This notion is examined with help from the Manchester United and English association football industry case study.

Once we have explored ten key ways of linking strategy and value, we then develop the concept of the 'business value system'. We define the business value system as being (see also Section 2.4):

'the system of internal *and* external value and cost drivers which determines, either directly or indirectly, the stream of cash flows within a business'.

Figure 2.1 thus represents the process.

Our definition of a 'value driver' is as follows:

'Anything either internal or external to a business which directly or indirectly contributes to *cash inflows*.'

Within 'value drivers' we include environmental factors such as the strength of customer demand for a product – and its perceived value within the customer value system. Also, we include indirect sources of value generation. For instance, a service delivered by, say, a finance or personnel department may not itself generate cash flows but it should certainly play a very specific *enabling* role in the cash generation of other business areas.

A 'cost driver' is now defined as being:

'Anything either internal or external to a business which directly or indirectly contributes to *cash outflows*.'

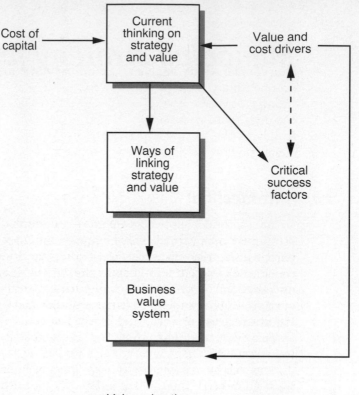

Figure 2.1   Managing for value

This might include, for example, the complexity of the product range, the extent to which customers are particularly demanding in relation to service, and the efficiency and effectiveness of the resource base. (See Chapter 7 on 'Strategic Cost Management' for a fuller treatment of the management of cost drivers.)

Finally, Figure 2.1 shows how outputs from the Business Value System lead on to strategies for value migration, which can be defined as being:

'The transition from increasingly outmoded business designs to ones which add more value to both customers and shareholders' (adapted from Slywotzky (1)).

For instance, as we see in the case study of Manchester United and the football industry later in this chapter (Case study 2.1), an industry can be rejuvenated by radical redesign. In the football industry this resided in adding more value for existing customers and adding value through new channels to market and to new customers. This has fundamentally reconfigured the football industry's value-creating activities during the 1990s.

The key sections of this chapter are thus as follows:

- shareholder value analysis, including value and cost driver analysis and beating the cost of capital (Section 2.2)
- linking strategy and value (and the tools of *Exploring Corporate Strategy* – our Section 2.3)
- exploring the 'business value system' (Section 2.4)
- conclusion and key questions (Sections 2.5 and 2.6).

2.2 *Shareholder value analysis*

2.2.1 *Value and cost drivers*

A number of writers have attempted to place finance in a strategic perspective. For instance, Rappaport (2) emphasises the need to consider the extent to which corporate and business strategy creates or destroys shareholder value. Rappaport suggests that during strategy-making we should explore the impact of key *value drivers* on the strategy.

Value drivers are both the internal and external underlying influences which generate present and future cash inflows. Value drivers can generate cash either directly or indirectly (in the latter case they may be produced by some internal service or other infrastructure).

Rappaport's core value drivers either focus mainly on internal factors or deal with the interface between the company and its environment. For instance, Rappaport lists:

- sales growth – this drives cash inflows and helps produce economies of scale
- competitive rivalry – is an indirect value driver. For example, acute competitive rivalry can often lead to discounting, price wars and severe reduction in margins
- margin is a most important value driver which follows on from competitive rivalry (and the company's own competitive strength in adding high value at low (relative) cost. As Rappaport points out, margin is particularly sensitive to the degree of competitive rivalry in the market.

Examples of value drivers in the grocery supermarket market (moving from internal to external) are:

- product mix (and margin)
- brand and service differentiation
- customer loyalty and price sensitivity

- the existence of 'soft' competitive targets (for example, newsagents, pharmacies, petrol stations)
- competitive rivalry.

2.2.2   Avoiding value destruction

To give a graphic illustration of how shareholder value analysis can be applied in practice, consider the following transaction. This occurred as a result of cancelling a mobile telephone network subscription. Illustration 2.1 shows how easily shareholder value can be destroyed as a result of competitive rivalry, company policy and customer behaviour.

Although Illustration 2.1 may seem an extreme example, there are countless other examples of where shareholder value is destroyed by

Strategy in action

illustration 2.1

Value destruction in the cellphone industry

Value can be destroyed not just at a macro level but at a micro level. Analysing micro level value destruction can give clues about what is happening at company and industry level.

After two and a half years of being connected to a major UK cellphone network, a self-employed businessman's cellphone neared the end of its life. Despite intensive testing by the manufacturer and one new battery, the cellphone (which had cost £200, new) worked for only five minutes before the 'Battery Low' message came on.

A convenient solution would have been for the businessman to have bought a new cellphone and connected the new handset to the existing network (which we will call 'Carephone'). However, this would have cost an additional £100 (at least) for a new telephone. Naturally, the businessman was inclined to avoid this cost if at all possible. Attracted by the special offers of the various networks, he disconnected the telephone and reconnected *a brand new telephone – with the same network, Carephone* for the sum of minus £10. There was no penalty for disconnection. This worked out as follows:

	£
Cost of new handset	20
Less trade-in on old model	(65)
Plus reconnection charge	35
Money paid to the businessman	(10)

On enquiry, the dealer informed him that his new telephone would normally cost £400 (being a superior model to the £100 ultra-cheap handset which he would have purchased if he had not disconnected from Carephone). The benefit to not managing the macro and micro value and cost drivers in the industry more effectively.

2.2.3 *Linking value and cost drivers with critical success factors*

Before we leave the topic of value and cost drivers for the present time, it is useful to clear up a possible confusion between these ideas and those of 'critical success factors'.

A definition of critical success factors is:

'Critical success factors are those aspects of strategy in which an organisation must excel to out-perform competition and are underpinned by core competences in specific activities or in managing linkages between activities.' (See *Exploring Corporate Strategy*, Section 4.6.2.)

Illustration 2.1 continued

him in making the switch was therefore between £110 and £410 depending upon the value put on the new telephone. (If he had not disconnected, he would have had precisely the same monthly network charge costs as before.)

His dealer also told him that his commission was £300 on this transaction.

The value destroyed within Carephone (relative to his not disconnecting) is therefore:

	£
New telephone*	400
Dealer commission	300
Value destruction	700

A very crude payback calculation on this value destruction, based on his new contract of £40 per month (including £20 per month of 'free' calls) is thus:

$$\frac{700}{40} = 17.5 \text{ months}$$

* We have assumed here that the handset price of £400 has minimal profit margin. Offsetting this simplified assumption is the assumption that the 'free' calls of £20 per month cost nothing to service.

To complete the picture, the dealer has profited to the tune of £300 (less variable costs). In summary, both the businessman and the dealer experienced value creation, whilst Carephone suffered major value destruction.

Now let us assume that this situation is by no means unusual and that many other customers decide to get rid of their ailing handsets around two to three years after purchase. Carephone (and the other competitors in the industry) will thus see a high proportion of their value added destroyed by this phenomenon, known in the industry as 'churn', manifest in lower margins.

Critical success factors are therefore *specific areas* in the business value system which managers need to focus on to achieve superior performance. For instance, to contrast a value driver with a critical success factor in a particular area we might have for a major supermarket chain:

Critical success factor
'To achieve a measurably superior customer service compared to our competitors through staff training and resulting behavioural change.'

Value driver
'The number of customers who defect from our competitors in seeing us as their preferred shopping destination.'

The critical success factor here is something quite specific which we must achieve *in order* to deliver enhanced value.

2.2.4   *Understanding the cost of capital*

Besides emphasising value drivers, the shareholder value theory (3) also promotes the notion of pursuing strategies whose cash flows will *exceed* the company's cost of capital. For instance, consider the following conglomerate group with three divisions consisting of leisure, property and retail.

Given the projected past tax cash flows of the business, the following profile emerges:

	Leisure	Property	Retail
Annual turnover of each division	£350m	£70m	£280m
Divisional cost of capital	12%	14%	13%
Present value of cash flows	£58m	(£12m)	£7m

Here, although the property division is relatively small (10 per cent of group turnover of £700 million), it destroys shareholder value. Retail is only just breaking even, whilst leisure is the powerhouse of shareholder value. This analysis might suggest that the property division is a candidate for turnaround or disposal. Also parts of the retail division may need a similar treatment.

The three main ways in which shareholder value analysis is helpful to strategic financial management are:

- it focuses on cash flow generation (sometimes called 'economic value added' or 'EVA' (3) as a key area for management focus

- it helps us to take into account the 'time value of money' when evaluating corporate and business strategies. (We will examine this issue further in Chapter 5.) Not only do *project* cash flows need to be discounted for this decline in value over time, but likewise *business* and *corporate* cash flows do also. Traditionally, managers have addressed the time value of money in project appraisal but may not have applied the techniques of discounted cash flow (DCF) at a higher, strategic level

- it stresses that conventional and historical measures of financial return (such as 'return on capital' as measured by both the profit and loss account and the balance sheet) can be misleading measures of financial performance. Because these accounting measures are based on non-cash adjustments and are typically derived from historic or one year's figures, they do not help us much when evaluating longer-term strategic options.

An example of the different effects of applying accounting measures of return on capital and of EVA-based measures is given in Illustration 2.2.

Different theorists have a range of views on the importance of accurate assessment of the cost of capital. For instance, Copeland et al (4) emphasise the need to obtain good estimates of the cost of capital. They prescribe setting different hurdle rates for different divisions where these divisions have different degrees of volatility relative to the stock market. (This is technically called 'systematic risk' to distinguish it from project-specific risk.) Whilst systematic risk identifies how project returns vary relative to the returns from investment opportunities available elsewhere to investors, project-specific risk is concerned with the inherent volatility of project cash flows.)

Whilst the overall cost of capital to a particular group may be, say, 13 per cent, different divisions (operating in different product/market segments) might have a cost of capital of 12 per cent, 14 per cent and even 15 per cent were they stand-alone businesses seeking external funding.

Copeland et al (4) regard the cost of capital as being one of *the most important* value drivers impacting on competitive strategy. Reimann (5) takes a different stance, suggesting that if we were realistic we would admit that many of the other value drivers are far more important and uncertain than the cost of capital. For instance, value drivers such as the level of competitive rivalry, the rate of growth in demand and the degree of organisational effectiveness are frequently more critical than the cost of capital.

Strategy in action

illustration 2.2

EVA analysis at Uniproduct Limited – an example

Measures of return on capital and of EVA (economic value added) can give very different pictures of the wealth generation of a business strategy. EVA is to be preferred as it focuses on cash flows – which are free from the distortions which accompany accounting-based measures.

Consider a single product business with a life of just three years. To calculate economic value added by the strategy, we have firstly identified the net cash flows from the business. We then adjust cash flows occurring in the future to reflect the time value of money – here 17 per cent (cash flows occurring at some future date are worth less than cash currently held due to a combination of the need to exact a return to cover risk and to allow for inflation).

Assumptions	Year 0 £'000	Year 1 £'000	Year 2 £'000	Year 3 £'000
1. Profit (after depreciation)		2,000	3,000	4,000
2. Capital employed		20,000	20,000	20,000
3. Depreciation		2,000	2,000	2,000
4. Working capital		3,000	3,000	3,000
5. Sale of plant (at net book value)				14,000
6. Return on capital calculation:				
Capital employed		20,000	20,000	20,000
Less Cumulative depreciation		(2,000)	(4,000)	(6,000)
Plus Working capital		3,000	3,000	3,000
		21,000	19,000	17,000
Return on capital 1) divided by 6)		9.5%	15.7%	23.5%

Giving an *average* return on capital over the three years of 16.2%

	Year 0 £'000	Year 1 £'000	Year 2 £'000	Year 3 £'000
7. Economic value added:				
Cash inflows (1 + 3)		4,000	5,000	6,000
Working capital recouped				3,000
Plant sold				14,000
		4,000	5,000	23,000
Cash outflows:				
Capital investment	20,000			
Working capital	3,000			
	23,000	–	–	–
Net cash flows	(23,000)	+4,000	+5,000	+23,000

Illustration 2.2 continued

Assumptions	Year 0 £'000	Year 1 £'000	Year 2 £'000	Year 3 £'000
Present value factor (cost of capital 17%)	$\dfrac{1}{1}$	$\dfrac{1}{1.17}$	$\dfrac{1}{(1.17)^2}$	$\dfrac{1}{(1.17)^3}$
Net cash flows x present value factor =	(23,000)	3,418	3,652	14,360

(Note: cash flows are assumed to occur at the end of years 1, 2 and 3.)

In the above, the sum of the present value of future cash flows from years 0 to 3 less initial outlays (known as the 'net present value' or NPV) is a negative £1.57 million. Thus whilst the investment appears to show an increasingly healthy return on capital, there is no positive present value. The business strategy thus *destroys shareholder value*.

In addition, the level of cost of capital at which the business achieves a (break-even) zero net present value, is approximately 13.7 per cent, as we prove as follows:

	Cash flows	Discount factor	Present value
Year 0	(£23,000)	$\dfrac{1}{1}$	(£23,000)
Year 1	4,000	$\dfrac{1}{1.137}$	3,518
Year 2	5,000	$\dfrac{1}{(1.137)^2}$	3,867
Year 3	23,000	$\dfrac{1}{(1.137)^3}$	15,647
	Net present value		32 (ie nearly zero)

This 'break-even' discount rate is called the 'internal rate of return'. Note that this internal rate of return of 13.7 per cent, which is an economic measure based on cash flows, gives a rather different impression of the business from the (accounting-based) return on capital employed of 16.2 per cent. Moreover, the impression of underlying profitability of the business is reinforced by the return on capital rising in year 3 to 23.5 per cent.

Accounting-based measures of performance are inferior to economic-based measures because they deal with hard cash flows – and not accrued income less expenses (or 'profit'). Certainly an investor would prefer to have £1,000 now rather than be owed £1,000 (to be in the future), where that debt had a zero interest rate, for that investor could reinvest the £1,000 to earn a return.

This example therefore makes a powerful argument for preferring economic-based measures of financial performance over accounting-based measures.

2.2.5   *Understanding the significance of shareholder value*

But identifying the cost of capital is perhaps a lesser issue compared to the need to integrate strategic and financial analysis. Regrettably the notion of 'shareholder value' over-emphasises the more technical and narrower *financial* analysis of business strategies. With relatively few exceptions it gives too little recognition to the need for a high degree of *strategic agility* in applying financial appraisal in valuing business strategies. Unless the detailed financial analysis is *preceded* by in-depth strategic analysis, then the result is likely to be 'Numbers Prevents Vision' (in other words a highly misleading net present value (or 'NPV').

There is a further issue here, too – from a *stakeholder perspective* – customers, staff and other external parties have an interest in how the value-creating activities of a company are conducted. Whilst 'shareholder value' is a most important concept – and indeed imperative for most businesses – it may not be overriding. Indeed, there are those who argue (like Anita Roddick of the Body Shop) that pursuing shareholder value as the dominant (if not exclusive) goal of a group may be in the long term harmful – both financially and non-financially.

The theory of shareholder value is sometimes accused of being overly and unnecessarily technical. For instance, the Head of Strategic Planning of Rolls-Royce Aeroengines in 1996, Simon Hart, had been involved in managing for shareholder value for over seven years:

> 'I find the literature very prescriptive, and not very helpful. All the original work by the theorists extolled the virtues of NPV (net present value) and said "this is great", but you know they glossed over the issues. For long product (and investment cycles) it [the theory] was very unhelpful.'

We redress this complaint by showing at a practical level how shareholder value needs to be managed in strategic investment decisions (Chapter 5), acquisitions (Chapter 6), and in cost (and change management) (Chapter 7).

2.2.6   *The hunt for value – guiding principles*

So how then should we balance the strategic and financial ingredients in 'Managing Strategy for Value'? Let us now set down three guiding principles:

- strategy and financial analysis are equal partners and neither one should dominate the other. Both forms of analysis are especially complementary in evaluating strategic decisions such as acquisitions, joint ventures and investment in new markets, products and distribution

- both strategic and financial analysis can be used to help creatively shape strategic development – this task is not solely or primarily that of strategic analysis

- we need to avoid the *deterministic* and *simplistic* notion that *all* the value of a business strategy or strategic project can be readily (and mechanistically) captured in the financial numbers.

Expanding first on the second above point, financial analysis can be used to trigger strategic questions about existing or new businesses which in turn lead to breakthrough ideas. Financial analysis can be invoked early on in the thinking process about options for strategic development, and not merely downstream at the business case stage. It may also be used to perform cross-company, cross-industry and cross-market niche comparisons of relative financial performance.

Turning next to our third guiding principle which concerns quantifying the value of a strategy, we *do not* assume that relatively uncertain value can always be translated into meaningful financials. There may well be situations where potential value exists but where this value is so dependent upon other factors (some of which being future) that value is at best illustrative. We call this value 'contingent value' to make it clear that it is best kept (and displayed) separately in any business case.

2.3   *Ways of linking strategy and value*

In this section we select ten strategy tools *specifically to relate competitive strategy to financial value.* These ten factors are subdivided into four groupings: strategic environment, business scope, competitive positioning and internal competitive advantage. (The section numberings refer to *Exploring Corporate Strategy* where a fuller treatment of the more purely *strategic* implications of these concepts is found.)

Strategic environment
- PEST (political, economic, social and technological) factors (Section 3.3.1).
- Growth drivers.
- The five competitive forces (6) (Section 3.3.2).

Business scope
- Mission (or 'strategic criteria') (Section 6.2.2).
- Business complexity and diversity (Section 6.2.3).

Competitive positioning
- Customer value analysis (Section 3.5.3).
- Competitor strategy (Section 3.5.5).

Internal competitive advantage
- Resource base analysis (Section 4.1).
- Core competences (Section 4.3).

2.3.1   Strategic environment

The 'strategic environment' of a company is crucial in determining its ultimate survival and success. Although it may be by now a truism that strategic environment is subject to change, whether this change is very slow and gradual, or sudden, turbulent and even life-threatening. PEST analysis helps managers to get a better handle on both current and impending changes.

PEST analysis is thus very far indeed from being a stand-alone strategic analysis tool. Not only does PEST analysis have a major and direct impact on financial value, but it also plays a profound role in influencing the very nature of competitive combat.

Moving closer into the factors of more immediate company impact, growth drivers are those influences within the market which are directly or indirectly helping to promote or sustain growth. 'Growth' here could mean growth generated through higher prices, higher volumes, or both. Growth drivers may be concerned with either the activation of demand (by converting new users) or through encouraging more use amongst existing users.

Analysing growth drivers is especially important because these are key underlying drivers of sales volumes and revenues, and are thus, indirectly, value drivers.

The five competitive forces (6) (see *Exploring Corporate Strategy*, Section 3.3.1) include:

- buyer power
- threat of entrants
- supplier power
- substitutes
- competitive rivalry.

Buyer power is concerned with the degree of discretion which customers have in choosing a supplier, in deciding whether or not and when to make a purchase, and their degree of influence over price, service and so on. 'Buyer power' is thus not a simplistic quality, but warrants a good deal of thought. A common failing is to assume that because there are very numerous, independent consumers, their bargaining power must be low. This may not be the case, for example in a retail market overlaid by recessionary conditions.

Unless there are few (and important) suppliers with special access to scarce resources or skills, then supplier power may be not so high – and not so influential. With the exception of those special cases

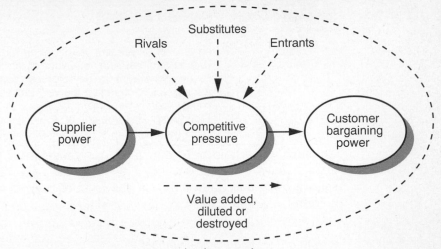

Figure 2.2   *The strategic environment – and value creation*

supplier power is probably not – on balance – as important as the other four competitive forces.

Substitutes, entrants and competitive rivalry generally (between existing players) can probably be grouped together as competitive pressure (see Figure 2.2). A common trap in dealing with substitutes is to define these from *the company's* perspective. An important health-check is to take the perspective of: imagine we are the customer – what are our needs and what alternative ways of meeting our needs exist?

We are now able to trace the key links between analysis and financial impact as follows (Table 2.1)

Table 2.1   *PEST analysis and financial impact*

Strategic analysis	Financial impact
• PEST factors	• Political: regulatory constraints close down opportunities for profitable development; or deregulation encourages rapid expansion of operators.
	• Economic: economic cycles either relax competitive conditions artificially or harden them unduly during recession. The financial effect is to generate volatile sales volumes, prices and margins – and restructuring costs.
	• Social: changes in social attitudes and life styles present new expansion opportunities (or opportunities for value-added and price increases), or close down suddenly lucrative opportunities.
	• Technological: technological developments open up new industry structures which encircle and make redundant

continued

Strategic analysis	Financial impact
	one's own, or present 'leapfrog' opportunities. Technology presents new ways of adding *more customer value* at the same or less cost, or delivering value quicker, changing the very basis under which competition is possible. Technology also impacts on the minimum level of investment to stay in the competitive game.

Although growth is only one factor to consider in evaluating the attractiveness of a market, it has nevertheless a significant impact on sales growth and (indirectly) on the level of competitive rivalry and margin (see Table 2.2).

Table 2.2   *Growth drivers and financial impact*

Strategic analysis	Financial impact
• Growth drivers	• High growth rates may require a high demand for investment – even just to maintain market share.
	• High volume growth may be accompanied by lower prices and thus margins.
	• Ultimately, profit will depend upon whether the business is concentrated on more inherently attractive areas or niches in the market. This 'inherent attractiveness' depends to a very large extent on the five competitive forces.

Turning next to the five competitive forces we now see (Table 2.3) the following picture:

Table 2.3   *The five competitive forces – and financial impact*

Strategic analysis	Financial impact
• Buyer power	• High bargaining power of buyers increases the costs of maintaining market penetration and customer base. It also increases costs of acquiring customers. It will also reduce the general price level and increase discounting.
• Supplier power	• High supplier power increases the costs of bought-in goods and services and makes discounts harder to obtain.
• Entrants, substitutes and competitive rivalry	• These competitive factors magnify the pressure on margins. They also increase the costs of having to continuously improve products and service delivery.

The five competitive forces thus play a profound role in dictating routes to competing successfully – and influence the resultant level of financial return.

2.3.2 Business scope

Table 2.4 now deals with the financial impact of the complexity of business scope (including complexity of mission and competitive strategy):

Table 2.4 *Mission, complexity and diversity of business scope – and financial impact*

Strategic analysis	Financial impact
•Mission	•Mission may act as too rigid a guide to strategy-making and implementation. This may result in untargeted and over-hardened strategic commitment. Operating managers may be committed to businesses which are inherently less attractive or with at best average competitive positions and thus relatively poor financial prospects. Only where mission/strategic intent capitalises on real synergies can it create rather than destroy value.
•Complexity and diversity of business scope	•The more complex the scope of business that one is in, the higher the costs are likely to be in switching resources from activity to activity. Also, complexity pushes up the costs of co-ordination and distraction costs as managers at the operating level have to deal with excessive diversity.

2.3.3 Competitive positioning

Besides identifying how much customer value is being currently created and captured, customer value analysis can also suggest major leap-frog opportunities – where it focuses on *future value* of customers. This future value can be identified by probing:

'What will add most value to the customer *in the future*?'

That is, by identifying the factors impacting on the customer in future (for instance, PEST factors, the five competitive forces and the industry mind-set). This can be particularly interesting in industrial markets where a deep understanding of the customers' present (and future) industry and of their likely *future* value system can yield significant insights. But this kind of analysis is not a very obvious theory to many managers. (This, paradoxically, is a *good thing* – because it may identify some important sources of future competitive advantage which other competitors are unlikely to have spotted.)

Illustration 2.3 now explores some of the dilemmas of assessing customer value based on the management consultancy industry.

Strategy in action

illustration 2.3
Evaluating the customer value of a management consultancy project

Many companies employ management consultants. But how would you put a value on their work? And how much would/should you be prepared to pay for it? These questions highlight some of the key practicalities of managing for value – how much value is created, by whom, and how is value shared out?

A management consultancy might be assisting a major company to transform itself from a slow-moving bureaucracy to a more responsive, leaner organisation. The benefits of this change might be felt through:

a) a lower cost base
b) loss of market share being avoided, and
c) new business ventures started.

The average annual benefits from the transformation exercise might be:

		£m
a)	Cost reduction	15
b)	Loss of market share avoided – net cash flows	20
c)	Starting new business ventures – net cash flows	5
		40 per annum

If we assumed that the benefits of the project would be felt primarily over a three-year period (and ignoring the time value of money – see Chapter 5), this gives us a cash benefit of £40 million annually.

Supposing we attribute a quarter of this breakthrough to the consultants (and three-quarters to management), the value of consulting input would be £120 million divided by 4, or £30 million. This calculation would be helpful to the consultants in justifying their £1 million fee (or 830 days of work at £1,200 a day) to their client – as a leverage of £30 benefit for every £1 spent.

In addition to customer value analysis, competitor analysis which integrates both financial and strategic analysis can give a much sharper view of their likely strategic intent. Rightly or wrongly, shorter-term financial performance exercises a profound influence over strategy-making at top management level. By thus examining financial prospects through a mind-set of a specific competitor, this gives a much clearer focus in anticipating competitor strategic intent. (See also Chapter 7 on 'Strategic Cost Management' for how to analyse a competitor's cost base.)

In summary, the impact of competitive positioning can thus be represented in Table 2.5.

Table 2.5   *Competitive positioning and financial impact*

Strategic analysis	Financial impact
•Customer value	•Identifies how much customer value is currently being created and harvested – through margins and discounts
	•Also can identify opportunities for enhancing future margins
•Competitor strategy	•Analysing competitor's strategy may identify areas of potential market share erosion (and thus lost revenues) or identify areas for attack (more revenues). Identifying where and how competitors make most money may help identify internal programmes to improve business and financial performance.

2.3.4   *Internal competitive advantage*

Finally, we turn to internal competitive advantage and to core competence and the resource base (see Table 2.6).

In conclusion, financial value is not only linked with competitive strategy but it can actually give the strategy a direct steer. Strategy is not only about the (qualitative) interplay of environment, competitive position and intent but requires a supporting financial analysis too. For financial analysis gives strategic analysis a more incisive bite,

Table 2.6   *Internal competitive advantage – and financial impact*

Strategic analysis	Financial impact
•Core competence	•Which competences add most value and which add least value? Which may actually dilute or destroy value? If competency is there on a just-in-case base, under what circumstances are they likely to be deployed, and will they then be too stale to actually capture value? Besides these value-related questions, one might also locate that competence which helps to *reduce cost*. (See the discussion of identifying competences which are hard to imitate in *Exploring Corporate Strategy*, Chapter 4.)
•Resource base	•The resource base not only enables competitive strategies to be pursued, but also drives the costs of the organisation.Where the resource base is inflexible and less flexible this drives up operating costs and also threatens restructuring costs during competitive change and recession.

particularly through analysing value drivers and the business value system.

We now develop the notion of the 'business value system' further, especially by relating it to the process of creating customer value.

2.4   *Exploring the business value system*

2.4.1   *The scope of the business value system*

Value is rarely generated in business through a single resource, but by resources combined together as part of a system. We call this system the 'business value system' (see *Exploring Corporate Strategy*, Section 4.3.1). This is represented in our Figure 2.3.

Figure 2.3 depicts a generic business unit as having a relatively flexible boundary (this is depicted as a dotted line). This highlights that the boundaries of modern businesses are frequently fuzzy. Specific competitors may choose to focus on particular parts of the industry value chain. This implies that there are frequently taken for granted choices about the resource and competence boundary of any business. Alliances open up a variety of options in re-configuring both the value chain and the supporting resource-base.

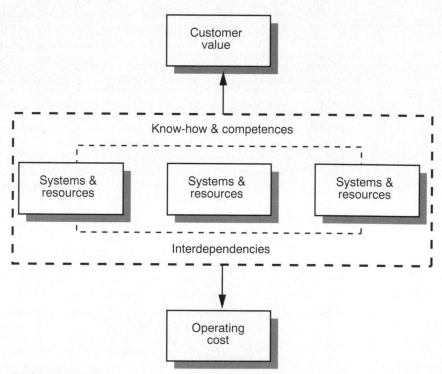

Figure 2.3   *The business value system*
Jointly developed with Cliff Bowman, of Cranfield School of Management

To explore the business value system we go through a number of steps:

- the customer perspective is our starting point
- motivators and hygiene factors drive customer value
- value creation is typically a non-linear process
- value creation does not necessarily mean value capture
- value systems need to migrate.

In order to illustrate the business value system we will be drawing from the case of Rolls-Royce Aeroengines and from Simon Hart, Head of its Strategic Planning Department.

2.4.2   *The customer perspective is our starting point*

We should now define 'value'. Value can be defined purely as price (the amount which a customer is being asked to pay). But in order to relate value to a customer-based perspective we have instead used the notion of 'Total Value' ('TV'). Total value is equal to Price plus Consumer Surplus. Total value is the amount a customer is prepared to pay for the product (see Figure 2.4).

Here 'Consumer Surplus' does not relate purely to the end-consumer, but may also relate to an intermediate consumer (in industrial markets). In both cases there is a use-value (to the customer) even if the product or service is subsequently transformed within a new (and intermediate) value system. But the missing ingredient in generating value here is *activities*. Resources do not in themselves add value, but only when they are deployed in activities through exploiting competences (see *Exploring Corporate Strategy*, Chapter 4).

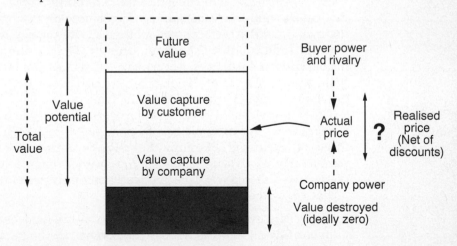

Figure 2.4   *Creating and capturing customer value*
Jointly developed with Cliff Bowman, of Cranfield School of Management

The resource base adds value through two separate groups of activities (see later our 'motivator' and 'hygiene' factors). This links into 'Resource Based Theory' within strategic management, which identifies a company's resources and core competences as being crucial in determining its longer-term business and financial performance. These activities generate use-value (for the customer) which in turn generates a consumer surplus.

The higher the use-value is perceived by the customer, then obviously the higher that Total Value becomes. Clearly we need to assess this value for differing market segments rather than attempt this on a whole market.

2.4.3 *Motivators and hygiene factors drive value*

An important clue in resolving problems of measuring value is the distinction between motivators and hygiene factors. This also enables us to explore the dynamics of value capture. (The idea of motivators and hygiene factors is imported from Hertzberg's (7) theory of motivation.)

Hygiene activities are those required to qualify for delivery of 'Perceived Use-value' (or 'PUV') from a customer perspective (see *Exploring Corporate Strategy*, Section 3.5.3). Where hygiene factors are not met they detract from value – and the buying impulse. Equally some activities may detract from the core delivery of value. Motivator activities excite customers, and are the sources of differentiation. It is likely that hygiene activities will (at best) just pass on their costs to total value. Motivators contribute more to total value. One way of distinguishing motivator activities from hygiene activities is to adapt Force Field Analysis ((9) and (10)) to the task.

In Figure 2.5 the conventional 'enabling' forces become the motivators, and the 'constraining' forces become the hygiene factors-not-met – and distractors. The relative size of the arrow (or vector) is a visual indication of the actual strength of indicators and hygiene factors (from a customers' perspective). This tool can be used either to help predict customer buying behaviour, or to perform customer bench-marking of value added by the firm.

One example of a motivator for aeroengines is superior engine performance. An example of a hygiene factor is safety. Simon Hart, Head of Strategic Planning Rolls-Royce Aeroengines explains a particularly motivating role of differentiated engine performance – distinctive reliability. This motivator actually encouraged a major airline to switch to Rolls-Royce:

> 'It is a rare event for customers to switch – we have had some switch in our favour, but it is a fairly rare event. In the particular case in point (of switching) it was because of the reliability. We have a very,

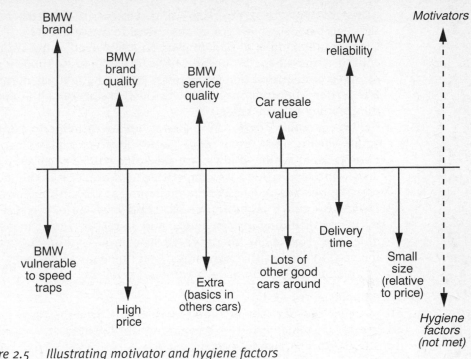

Figure 2.5 *Illustrating motivator and hygiene factors – BMW car bought by a businessman*

very reliable one. And this particular customer – because there was a lot of night flying involved, and it had to get in and out with a very high level of despatch reliability, he actually chose to switch from a competitor's products to ours.'

The pattern of motivators and hygiene factors is specific to a customer (in relation to a particular supplier). As this pattern alters considerably between even individual customers this explains why, even when a firm offers very high use-value, but at a relatively low price, still some customers will buy from elsewhere. It also underlies the importance of building and reinforcing customer-specific motivator activities – to discourage switching.

2.4.4 *Value creation is often a non-linear process*

Resources do not and will not add value in a linear way as they are applied in progressive amounts. This is because of the complexity of the business value system. For example we might initially experience low returns for an investment after a period and then suddenly, once a step-change in motivator factors has been achieved, a sweeping increase of returns occurs. In certain industries where there are increasingly complex business value systems, it is hardly surprising that companies experience as the reward for a build up of effort and competence, sudden and disproportionate returns (or as Waldrop (11) calls it – increasing returns). Microsoft's Windows 1995 is a classic example of disproportionate returns, producing a super-normal profit stream for Microsoft in 1996. (Obviously, sometimes the opposite of *diminishing returns* holds.)

For example, Figure 2.6 explores an investment to reposition a small theme park from being a minor attraction to becoming a national one. Adding a few more rides (like the ones already existing) does relatively little to its competitive advantage. But the addition of possibly two new rides (like the major one at UK's Alton Towers – The Nemesis – which is guaranteed to thrill even an experienced theme park goer including my son James and daughter Nicole) makes all the difference. Notice how there is a 'turbo-charge' type of effect of a major increase in competitive advantage – on financial advantage.

This increase in financial advantage is felt in:

a) a higher entry fee
b) more volume of customers (and more evenly over the year)
c) greater customer loyalty – second and third visits
d) a higher proportion of secondary sales.

Again, it is the *cumulative* effect of a) to d) which is the reward for a breakthrough in competitive advantage.

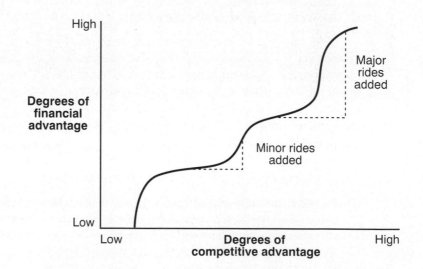

Figure 2.6   Linking degrees of competitive and financial advantage – a theme park

2.4.5 *Value creation does not necessarily mean value capture*

The split of value captured by customer versus supplier is determined by the bargaining arrangements (and level of co-operation) between both parties. (See Figure 2.4 again.) This links closely with Porter's five competitive forces. The main point here (often missed by managers) is that theoretical value creation does not necessarily equate with value capture. For example, you might assume that you will sell a certain number of aeroengines at a certain set price because they do have distinctive benefits. However, an aggressive buyer may strive to capture virtually all this extra value through his control over the buying process. Simon Hart of Rolls-Royce illustrates the influence of value sharing as follows:

> 'By the way he negotiates a deal, he (the customer) will say, I, the customer want value, and the way that I will abstract value from the system is to run a competition, and obviously that drives certain decisions throughout the whole supply chain.'

2.4.6 *Business value systems may need to migrate*

Where a customer's pattern of motivator/hygiene requirements is shifting, or where the supplier's total offering (including the relationship) is changing, a customer will scan more and more actively, and wider and wider, for alternative supply. This search activity (combined with competitor activity) causes 'distraction' to build up within the customer, reinforcing the significance of any hygiene factors not fully met.

As mentioned earlier, motivator factors will generally tend to become hygiene activities with the passing of time. This migration is caused through competition and the effects of imitation.

Figure 2.7 shows how this can develop dynamically over time. As the industry evolves companies seek to migrate their business value systems. This can occur by a combination of divestment, out-sourcing, value-system simplification, acquisition and new start-ups. The situation of Rolls-Royce Aeroengines graphically illustrates this. Simon Hart applies this concept to Rolls-Royce's core business activities:

> 'Engineering and manufacturing people have been working together, asking questions like "which components do we actually have to be making and designing, because they are fundamental to the integrity of the product?"'

This means you may wish to migrate the way in which you add value to a new business value system (or perform 'value migration') (1). Value migration may involve dropping activities which offer less

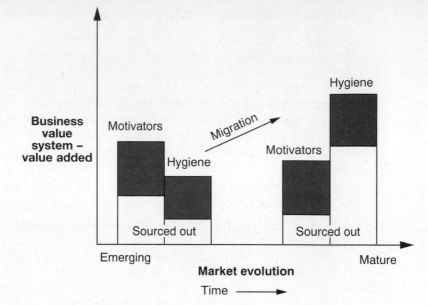

Figure 2.7   *Migrating the business value system*
Developed in conjunction with Cliff Bowman

and less motivator potential and continual re-thinking of hygiene activities so that these are achieved at a lower and lower cost. This migration imperative clearly determines the selection of which activities to focus on. Simon Hart elaborates:

> 'Some parts are important to the integrity of the engine. Broadly speaking, the hot section is crucial to the operations... Obviously if you felt you had a competitive range in a particular technology, then you would retain the technology. But there is a choice as to whether you make all of this – which part you make and which you off-load, and then you have to step down these (parts) categories.'

Value migration is a much more fundamental thing than simple re-engineering business processes. Migrating value may involve withdrawal from some value-creating activities *in toto*, or identifying completely new ones.

Now we have examined the main themes of managing for value we will use Manchester United and the football industry to illustrate the rich interplay between these themes; we will particularly focus on the business value system. Manchester United is an example of how *four factors* have combined to generate super-normal profits and economic value generation for its shareholders. The first factor is the deliberate creation of an inherently attractive market (Porter's five forces and growth drivers). Secondly, the *value domain* of the football industry has been extended to incorporate retail, media and leisure-based activities. (The value domain is the scope of value-creating activities.) Thirdly, Manchester United has established a very strong competitive position. Fourthly, it has *aligned* its business value system externally and internally to achieve disproportionate value.

Case study 2.1

Manchester United and the Association Football industry

The football industry is one which has traditionally added value in simple ways but which has changed into one which is complex, changing the basis of competing. This case study is set out as follows:

- The strategic situation of the industry? (Case Study 2.1)
- Strategy, value and football – at Manchester United
  – an illustration (Illustration 2.4).

2.1.1 The strategic situation of the football industry

As a prelude to our case study, we examine the nature of football as an industry, industry change and then the position of Manchester United.

Association Football ('soccer') is the most popular spectator sport in Britain, with six times more attendance than the next most popular sports – greyhound racing and horse racing. Football is also received with similar enthusiasm in many European countries – and indeed worldwide, where frequently the level of excitement generated exceeds that in the UK.

Summarising a five forces analysis:

- buyers have a relatively low bargaining power (as their loyalty to clubs in traditional customer segments is usually very high). This loyalty is breaking down as an increasing proportion of followers watch different teams.
  This force historically supports above-normal value creation in the industry, but this effect may disappear

- suppliers do have considerable (high) bargaining power – these suppliers being particularly the players. Players' salaries absorb typically *over half* of gate takings and high-performing players command considerable transfer fees.
  This force may thus undermine value creation in the industry

- substitutes are an important threat. We include here direct substitutes such as other leisure activities, besides indirect substitutes, such as watching games on satellite television.
  This force thus poses a threat to value creation

- competitive rivalry: oddly there is not typically an intense rivalry for fans on a local basis, although rivalry on the pitch is high. The 'rivalry' force does not act to depress industry profits in a serious way.
  This force thus plays a neutral or even positive role in supporting value creation

This competitive forces analysis suggests that, although the competitive environment generally supports a super-normal value creation in the industry, there are significant longer-term threats to this. Further, past, recent (and anticipated) growth trends may be largely responsible for investors seeing this industry as generally 'attractive' (ie offering superior returns) and future and (untested) possibilities of further value generation through pay-for-view televised matches.

But before we move onto how the business value system is evolving, let us take a closer look at how these 'super-normal' profits are distributed in the industry.

Surprisingly, perhaps, the football industry is not traditionally a very profitable one overall. In 1993/94, for instance, during a time of recession, English professional football as an entire industry reported a pre-tax profit of just £12,000 on turnover of £387 million. But what is even more impressive is the performance of a very small number of clubs, for instance, Manchester United and Arsenal. In 1993/94 the top eight clubs made a combined pre-tax profit of £25.5 million, and the rest made a substantial loss.

The strongest group of clubs (known sometimes in strategic management as a 'strategic group' (see *Exploring Corporate Strategy* Section 3.5.1)) have exploited – and some would say over-exploited – their merchandising.

This phenomenon in turn raises some issues about the *sustainability* of the merchandising strategies of clubs like Manchester United (see Illustration 2.4, coming shortly). If it is no longer so trendy to be seen walking around with Manchester United's latest replica strip (which changes periodically), this could pose a major threat to both the volumes and margins of merchandising operations. (In 1996, *Verdict* reported that the football merchandising market stood at £150 million, or approximately 3.7 million strips per annum at an average price of £40, suggesting near-market saturation. Indeed, the conventional market for children's clothes shrunk by 2 per cent in 1996 due to this substitution effect. But what might happen if this trend were to reverse? – see again our Section 2.3.1 on growth drivers.

Football has therefore now developed from its traditional base of taking receipts for the game to a much more complex set of business activities, for example sponsorship, advertising, television, merchandising, conferences and catering, extending its value domain.

Strategy in action

illustration 2.4

Strategy, value and football – at Manchester United

Football has been transformed from an industry with relatively low value creation to one with high value creation – for Premier League clubs. By migrating the way in which value has been created in the industry, Manchester United has achieved extraordinary returns for its shareholders.

Manchester United has been a very successful football club for several decades. It has thrived despite setbacks – for example, the Munich air crash of 1958 which effectively wiped out the team. In the 1960s it spawned players like Bobby Charlton and George Best, and under Alex Ferguson, its manager, has rekindled this success in the 1990s.

Manchester United has been instrumental in changing the game from being primarily a spectator activity to a mass, market-based product. This has transformed its financial results.

Financial analysis of the breakdown of the club's turnover over the last few years highlights the changing businesses in which larger football clubs are involved. Figure 2.8 shows how the revenue of Manchester United has grown since 1989: all categories of revenue have grown but that from merchandising has shown the greatest increase. The top graph demonstrates how the total revenue split has changed since 1989: the decrease in the proportion of revenue coming from gate receipts and the growth of the revenue from merchandise pre-tax can be clearly seen. By 1995 profits stood at £20 million, dwarfing Glasgow Rangers' £7.1m, Barcelona's £8.5m, and Real Madrid's £3m.

2.1.2   Value-creating activities

First of all we look at:

- value creation in the football industry – and at Manchester United
- industry change and value creating activities
- cost drivers and competitiveness
- alternatives for future industry change and for Manchester United.

Value is created in any business through the interaction of a number of external and internal factors which we call the 'business value system'. Besides the traditional value-creating activities of fans paying to see their team in action, the years 1994 to 1997 saw a huge growth in football merchandising.

This merchandising includes, for instance, Manchester United replica strips which cost anything between £30–£45 for children, and up to over £60 for adult strips. These strips appear to command a considerable premium relative to other fashion items.

A business value system for the successful football clubs is shown in

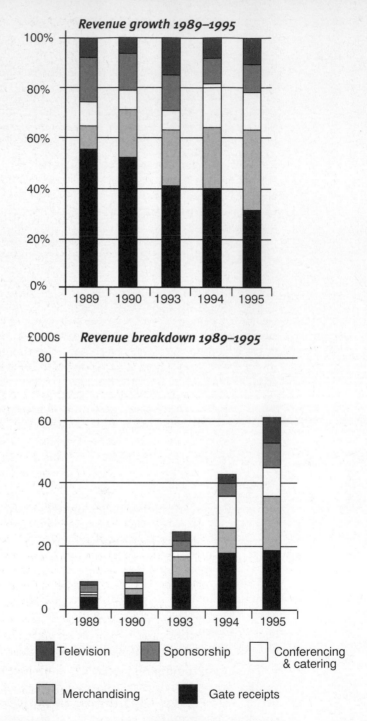

Figure 2.8   Manchester united revenue growth and breakdown 1989 – 1995

Figure 2.9. This highlights the need to maintain match performance as a means of providing the platform for value-creating activities elsewhere. It is precisely because of the *interdependencies* within this business value system that you cannot naively answer the question of 'Exactly where do we make (or lose) money in our (football) business?' (Football, of course, is not unique in this – most business interdependencies make value measurement very difficult to achieve.)

This question is also linked to the adjacent one of:

'Where (and how) will we make money in the future?'

Although this is a question implicit in most treatments of strategy formulation, in practice this question is very much at the forefront of managers' minds.

For example, if we focus once again on the situation of Manchester United, some very major pressures on its drive towards game commercialisation have emerged. This has provoked a backlash from sections of the traditional fan base, who have actually demanded seats on the board. The Prime Minister, Tony Blair, has actively criticised (before he came to power) the extremes to which the industry has gone to exploit the game. In a different political scenario

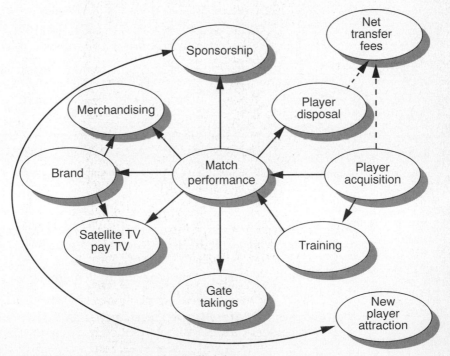

Figure 2.9   Business value system – football clubs

to the current state of affairs, Manchester United could find it difficult (or impossible) to sustain its very profitable UK merchandising operation.

Interestingly, there is evidence that the club has anticipated this scenario – or one like it. For instance, *The Times* – Sport (10 February 1996) reported that United signed up a deal worth £60m with a sponsor Umbro (over six years).   This partnership gave United access to the Far East and Japanese markets, giving United the beginnings of a world market.

In the future it is likely that media coverage will prove an increasingly important source of revenue. Manchester United has now decided to set up its own Sky satellite channel. Also, revenues from European matches are expected to increase considerably. This has been a major factor in increasing the club's market capitalisation (amongst bid rumours) to a healthy half a billion pounds by late 1996. A summary of how Manchester United as an organisation now adds value (and potentially destroys value), and to whom, is as follows:

Table 2.7   *Manchester United stakeholder value*

Stakeholders	Value added	Value destroyed
Fans	• Match spectating • Merchandising available	• Hard to get in (tickets are rationed) • Over-expensive merchandising?
Players	• Career development	• High salaries and transfer fees
Managers	• Profit sharing • Salaries	• None
Merchandisers	• Sales of kit	• None
Media	• Media revenues	
Shareholders	• Share price rises • Dividends/profits	• Share price falls

(Note: 'value creation' means either positive cash flow or the creation of other, less tangible value to the shareholder.)

The above list highlights the tensions that might arise in managing the club, for example between:

- the interests of players (in securing high salaries) versus managers and shareholders (profits)

- the interests of media versus the club in dividing up television and satellite revenues

- the interests of management and shareholders in balancing shorter-term profits against longer-term shareholder value.

On the final point above, the *Sunday Times* (28 April 1996) highlighted the volatility of Manchester United's share price (which bobbed up and down around 100p a share between 1993 and 1994 and then shot up to 200p in 1995 and then 480–500p in 1996). For instance, when leading player Cantona assaulted a Crystal Palace fan in 1995 (leading to his ban from football for many months), its share price fell 5 pence. Manchester United's share price appears particularly volatile to the short-term performance of the team.

2.1.3   Value drivers

If we now look more generally, value is created in any business through the interaction of a number of external and internal factors. These combine to generate cash flow either directly or indirectly. At Manchester United an obvious ingredient is the ability to win match after match, or to come back after set-backs. Indeed, one speculated (prior to the 1996/1997 season) whether a series of bad playing performances might result in a loss of interest in the club and a fall-off in its new source of income and cash flow. For example, in autumn 1996, Manchester United suffered a series of unparalleled defeats both in the Premier League and European Cup, but still went on to win the League.

Strategically, the industry was not helped initially by external regulatory pressure (linking back to our PEST factors in Section 2.3). An external report on ground safety (*The Taylor Report*) led to grounds installing all-seater stadia, costing £282 million. Going to a football match today is a serious financial investment, especially because the all-seater grounds have a substantially reduced capacity relative to the older, squashed-in arrangements. On the other hand, this has removed hygiene factors not-being-met of the need for fans to feel physically secure – and has thus helped bring about a widening of the market.

To date, media activities have not been the pot of gold which one might have expected. The media companies have managed to exert quite strong buyer power and negotiated relatively favourable contracts. The future of football broadcasting will obviously have a very big impact on the business value system of the various clubs. The clubs are now trying to reverse things.

Returning to the issue of commercialisation of the clubs, especially merchandising, it is hard to see how the leading clubs can enhance their existing earnings streams (except in new media revenues – for example, through pay-per-view television). For instance, in 1995, gate receipts and programme sales amounted for the first time ever in the club's history to less than half of total turnover, which itself grew by 38 per cent over the year. Tottenham Hotspur also saw operating profits for their merchandise, such as replica kits, jump 78 per cent in 1995. But is this growth sustainable?

The merchandising life cycle may be shorter than imagined since the target market is relatively discrete. It is estimated at Newcastle United, for example, another club that has been extremely successful at developing merchandising activities, that some 75 per cent of their regular attenders at matches now own a Newcastle strip. Incremental gains, it is recognised, will therefore become ever more difficult, and maybe revenues will reverse.

If we now focus on the key value drivers of Manchester United we see that they fall into a number of interrelated clusters. These consist of:

- Merchandising
- Media
- Match takings
- Effectiveness of play.

Merchandising value drivers include:

- the continued strength of the Manchester United brand (which depends partly on the effectiveness of play)
- the popularity of football generally
- the strength of the fashion
- football strips' role in the gift market.

Media value drivers include:

- the total fees for coverage of Premier League games
- the growth drivers of the 'pay-per-view' satellite TV market.

Match takings are dependent upon the following value drivers:

- the Manchester United brand
- the effectiveness of play
- fan loyalty
- the number of European games played (which pay £1 million extra *per game*)
- the effectiveness of selling additional services
- ground capacity.

The effectiveness of play underpins the other value driver clusters. It is dependent upon:

- the amount of money spent on acquiring top-class players (although this is not always spent well)

- their degree of compatibility with the existing and future team make-up, and with the culture of the club and the national game
- the club's ability to assimilate, to train and develop new players
- the incidence of injury or absence (through missing matches because of cumulative penalty points)
- the ability of the team to play as a team – as being more than the sum of its players.

(We can make some interesting comparisons between football team play and the role of the *human resource* in adding value to companies. It is sometimes hard to measure the *individual* contribution by specific managers and staff generally to value generation. Nevertheless, their collective performance plays a decisive role.)

The role of actually scoring a goal is an interesting issue, for goal scoring is a tangible value driver, leading to winning games. In spring 1997, Manchester United failed to score a single goal in the second leg of the European Cup Quarter-Final despite having over a dozen excellent chances. In the same way, in other businesses, performance within the business value system which *almost but doesn't quite reach the levels of fulfilling customer value expectations* means that economic value fails to crystallise.

2.1.4   *Changes in cost drivers – and industry change*

Turning next to cost drivers, in the 1990s there has been an undeniably increasing pressure on clubs' costs. The transfer market, for example, is growing fast. In 1994-95 £110 million was spent on player transfers (compared with £73 million in 1992-93). Alan Shearer, bought by Newcastle United for £15 million in 1996 could (if his cost were spread over, say, seven years and forty games or so per season) cost around £50,000 per game, and £65,000 per goal.

One might well speculate how this value was arrived at. It would be very difficult to do a straightforward NPV for Alan Shearer as his value is influenced by uncertainty, interdependencies, and by 'intangibles' (see Chapter 5 for a treatment of these three problem areas). However, this does illustrate the feature of value-creation occurring in a non-linear fashion.

For example, if buying Alan Shearer had made the difference between Newcastle qualifying/not qualifying for a European competition in 1997/98, this might have been worth £5 million or so (each match is estimated to be worth £1 million extra profit). This did subsequently occur.

This trend is likely to continue as top clubs compete more for 'big signings' and a higher premium must be paid for star quality. The growing transfer market has also more importantly sparked wage rises and the recent transfer ruling allowing greater freedom of movement for players will accelerate this trend as clubs compete for players with wages. Players' earnings rose generally by 19 per cent in 1993–94 and this trend will certainly continue. (In 1996, Manchester United spent an extra £5 million on players' salaries resulting in a short-term profits dip.)

At the same time, major investments have been made to grounds and have consumed capital. Continued investments will need to be made but there is a danger that certain clubs will 'feel richer' and fuel the transfer market further. Perhaps, at some stage, the 'bubble' will burst unless revenues are fuelled by pay-per-view TV.

We now briefly describe a scenario where pressure mounts on football clubs to revise or moderate their 'commercialisation' strategy and they are left with falling revenues and margins at a time of unduly high costs. The likely result: fall-out of weaker clubs (and maybe even financial failure of one or more of the larger clubs is a scenario with at least some plausibility. The 'end-game' here would be literally restructuring the game. Indeed, the *Sunday Times* (11 February 1996) highlights one possible new development – a super six-a-side league with the very top players, shorter pitches and even a six-a-side world club (a 'new industry').

2.1.5   *Alternatives for future value creation?*

With its rivals hot on its heels, Manchester United might feel under pressure to sustain the success of recent years. We now pose a number of questions (for the reader to think about) for the Manchester United Board and for further debate:

- to what extent is the success of Manchester United's merchandising strategy likely to be sustainable in the future (for example, will it prove to be a fashion and vulnerable to life-cycle effects)? What might this do to that most important value driver, margins?
- how might Manchester United develop its brand and merchandising further (for example, internationally)? Where will this give a sustained margin advantage and/or incremental volume?
- if Manchester United were acquired by another leisure-based company, what value would the new parent add, and how might this affect Manchester United's strategic intent?
- how will the influence of the *media* shape the industry, and how can Manchester United influence the course of development of football on TV (terrestrial and satellite, or the Internet)? What cash streams would occur?
- what changes in the political or social environment might change the industry (for example, how might a different government influence public attitude to exploiting the game commercially)?
- how might the game itself evolve (for example, towards a European super league)? How would you design this so as to maximise value generated?

2.1.6   Key lessons from the football case study and Manchester United illustration

The key lessons from this case study on managing for value are:

- it is impossible to appreciate fully the factors driving an industry – both now and future – without an appreciation of both the strategic drivers and how financial value is being created in the business value system

- in order to identify the possibilities for value migration, we must work backwards from current and latent customer value. What are the 'motivators' which might cause a customer to re-evaluate perceived value? And how can a reasonable element of this extra perceived value be captured by the company (for example, through a higher price)?

- besides asking the question 'where should we go strategically?' we have to ask – simultaneously – 'where and how will we be making money?'. The notion that financial analysis 'brings up the rear' – and only follows on from strategic analysis, is most dangerous and misleading

- effective co-ordination of strategic and financial performance requires skilful balancing and trade-offs, rather than a pursuit of particular financial goals to the exclusion of more indirect impact. In the football industry we saw just how fragile an apparently effective competitive and financial strategy (medium-term) could be longer-term

- superior financial performance is very much contingent upon creating and preserving an external competitive environment which is *conducive* to making good returns. This profit-earning potential is then amplified by competitive dominance (as at Manchester United), and is then underpinned by layer-upon-layer of reinforcing competitive advantage. But it is also contingent upon implementing the strategy with effective implementation (or put plainly, 'getting it absolutely right'); this does play a very major role in determining critical financial returns

- although it may be difficult, it may be possible to put a value on organisational competence. For example, if one can put a value on a player (and their distinctive skill), then the same applies to the organisation.

(Input for this case study was derived from an MBA project by Sophie Castell, Keith Taylor and Julian Watson in 1996.)

2.5   Conclusion

We have now demonstrated the importance of managing strategy for value as a major theme in strategic management. We will next be examining more closely how this can be made a reality in both future decision-making (or in 'Strategic Management Accounting' -Chapter 3) and in understanding past and current financial performance (or in 'Strategic Financial Accounting' – Chapter 4).

But, most importantly, we have seen how managing strategy for value is applicable not merely at the industry level, or indeed the company level, but also in managing particular company policies at a micro level.

2.6   Key questions

Now you have covered the elements of managing strategy for value you should consider the following key questions:

1. What are the main *internal* value drivers within your business?
2. What are the main *external* value drivers outside your business?
3. How do those value drivers interact with one another? (We suggest you try to represent this pictorially, perhaps by drawing arrows to represent the key interdependencies.)
4. How *might* you manage them more effectively than at present?
5. In particular, to what extent do you need to migrate your business value system to improve your competitive advantage and to deliver distinctive competitive value?

References

(1) Slywotzky J., *Value Migration*, Harvard Business School Press, 1996
(2) Rappaport A., *Creating Shareholder Value*, The Free Press, New York, 1986
(3) Stewart G. B., *The Quest for Value*, Harperbusiness, 1991
(4) Copeland T., Koller T., Murrin J., *Valuation – Measuring and Managing the Value of Companies*, John Wiley and Sons, 1990
(5) Reimann B., *Managing for Value: A Guide to Value-Based Strategic Management*, Basil Blackwell, Oxford, 1990
(6) Porter E. M., *Competitive Strategy: Techniques for Analysing Industries and Competitors*, The Free Press, New York, 1980
(7) Hertzberg F., *The Motivation to Work*, John Wiley and Sons, New York, 1959
(8) See *Exploring Corporate Strategy*, Section 3.5.3
(9) Lewin K., *A Dynamic Theory of Personality*, McGraw Book Company, New York, 1935
(10) Grundy A. N., *Breakthrough Strategies for Growth*, Pitman, 1995
(11) Waldrop M. M., *Complexity*, Penguin Books, 1992

3 Strategic management accounting

3.1 Introduction

When most managers hear the words 'management accounting', the typical association of ideas is probably:

'Standard costing, overhead allocation, break-even analysis.'

Whilst these techniques certainly have their role to play, they often suffer from setting up expectations that decision-making can be turned into a relatively precise and accurate quantification exercise. Moreover, the techniques assume that there is a straight-line relationship between changing one variable (for example, selling more of a new product) and another (for example, increasing economic profit). But value is not always created in business in direct proportion to an increase in activity.

So, it should not really come as a complete shock that we see *strategic* management accounting in a rather different light – where quantification is merely seen as one of several important ingredients in decision-taking.

Strategic management accounting (SMA) can thus now be defined as:

'An integrated framework for strategic and financial decision-making and for interpreting business performance which brings together competitive, operational and financial analysis.'

Strategic management accounting is differentiated from traditional management accounting through:

- being genuinely integrated conceptually (rather than being a set of disparate techniques)
- bringing together strategic and financial decision-making within the same thought process
- showing clearly and specifically how competitive, operational and financial analysis tools are applied together.

Dealing effectively with business complexity requires *the simplest* framework we can devise, rather than the most complex. Basically, strategic management accounting is about analysing business *data* to help cope with strategic and financial *dilemmas* and ultimately to make *decisions* which do not end in too many unpleasant *disappointments* or *disasters* (our five d's).

We now need to outline some of the key challenges facing strategic management accounting, and also how those challenges can be approached. This is done by examining some key content issues which are addressed in the Strategic Management Accounting Framework.

Following the content issues, we then address process issues and SMA reports and accounting techniques. We then conclude with an illustration of SMA-based thinking with Virgin Direct – Rejuvenating the Financial Services Industry – a case study.

3.2   *Strategic management accounting – a framework*

The key ingredients of Strategic Management Accounting are represented in Figure 3.1 (1).

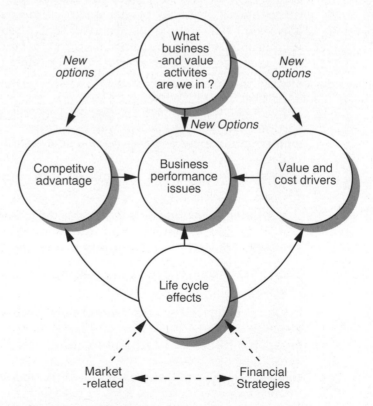

Figure 3.1   Strategic management accounting

The six key ingredients of SMA are:

- the definition of 'what business(es) we are in' and the business design – or portfolio analyses in Figure 8.2 of *Exploring Corporate Strategy* (see our Section 3.3)
- the major life-cycle effects (2)
- the assessment of competitive advantage – or 'suitability' and positioning in Figure 8.2 (see our Section 3.5)
- the value and cost drivers – or value chain analysis of Figure 8.2 (which we already addressed in Chapter 2 – Managing Strategy For Value)
- the new options – for value creation (3)
- the key performance issues - or 'business profile' from Figure 8.2 (see our Section 3.7).

Each of these six elements is closely interdependent with each of the others. For instance, the business design needs to be understood as a framework for assessing competitive advantage. Equally, the value drivers underpin competitive advantage and will be a reflection of the business design.

The 'new options' are shown in Figure 3.1 as being generated out of reflecting on 'what business are we in (could we be in)?', on changes in competitive advantage, and from understanding existing (and new) value and cost drivers.

Performance issues are then addressed by a combination of asking what business you are in, by examining competitive advantage or disadvantage, or the functioning of the value drivers. Finally, life-cycle effects will shape competitive advantage, the key value and cost drivers, and resulting business performance.

We begin therefore by examining the issue of 'what business are we in?', before turning to the impact of competitive advantage on the value drivers. We then reflect on life-cycle effects before dealing with performance issues.

Before applying strategic management accounting we should ask ourselves the question of 'what are we trying to account for?' This inevitably leads on to the question 'what business are we in?' So before we can begin to understand and manage business performance more effectively we first need to address 'what business are we in?'

Exploring Corporate Strategy addresses the issue of 'what business are we in?' at a portfolio level. But within a particular business unit there will be a variety of *types* of business which need analysing as part of the SMA process.

3.3   *What business are we in?*

When we ask ourselves the question 'What business(es) are we in?'

(and also 'what value do they add?'), invariably we are left dealing with a fair degree of complexity. Even where a business is said to be following a 'focus strategy' this may often disguise a somewhat complex set of businesses beneath it. For instance, in Table 3.1 we contrast a number of 'focused' businesses.

Where a company *has not* adopted a 'focus' strategy (or we might say in the above examples, a 'stretched focus' strategy), then business complexity soon multiplies – almost exponentially. This can easily result in dilution of shareholder value.

The question of 'what business are we in?' can be tackled by examining the three major dimensions of the business (see Table 3.1), especially:

a) its products and services
b) its customer types and their needs
c) its markets (including delivery channels).

Besides its current design, any business also has a past and a future potential design. There are also business areas to which we have a low, medium or high commitment. (Some of this commitment might be misplaced.) These levels of commitment may be high or low to enter a new business area. They may also be high or low relative to an *existing* business.

There are also variations in our state of knowledge about what does (and does not) make money in the business – and what are its key values and cost drivers. On top of this is the dimension of *difficulty*: how easy or how difficult is it to make money in a particular business? This is a different dimension to inherent financial attractiveness. We can have a business which is relatively lucrative (for example, doing major management consultancy projects for blue chip companies undergoing corporate transformation) but which is hard to deliver

Table 3.1   *Understanding focus strategies*

Business	Focus	Breadth
BMW: cars	•Sporty, prestige cars.	•Many customer segments and increasingly broad product range.
Marks & Spencer: retail	•Relatively narrow range of products.	•Broad customer appeal.
First Direct: banking	•Telephone banking, higher income customers, simple products.	•Relatively broad product coverage.

effectively. Or, we might have businesses where it is both possible to make money *and* (at least at the present time), easily. We examine this trade-off in more depth in Chapter 5.

3.4 Life-cycle analysis

In this section we first consider how life-cycles affect the core issues which strategic management accounting concerns itself with. This is then followed by a sub-section on the impact life-cycles have on *future* financial strategy. Although the financial strategy issues are related to *external* requirements (to service shareholders) these issues need to be addressed in parallel with the internal effects of life-cycles, as they are closely interrelated.

Exploring Corporate Strategy (Section 8.2) asks: 'Does it (the business) fit the stage we will be in?' So how can strategic management accounting help us to judge the fit of our corporate life-cycle stage with the life-cycle of a business or sub-element of a business?

3.4.1 Life-cycle effects and strategic management accounting

To address this question we need to explore the impact of dynamic effects, both in terms of conventional market life-cycle analysis and also in terms of degrees of competitive advantage. Both life-cycle effects and competitive advantage can also be related to financial performance as we now see.

Conventional life-cycle analysis suggests a number of stages which run more or less sequentially over time: emerging, growth, maturing, decline, renewal.

In each stage there is likely to be a different focus of attention in strategic management accounting, which we see in Table 3.2. The first question here is: what stage are particular elements of our products/markets at (generally)? We can then judge the extent to which a particular business area reflects or is out of character with our life-cycle profile.

Table 3.2 highlights a typical set of priorities in each of the five product life-cycle phases. In the 'emerging' phase the main focus typically will be on revenue planning, with product profitability coming second and the other factors third.

In the 'growth' phase revenue planning is still of high importance but this is more balanced by product and customer profitability. Moving into 'maturity' we see the situation reversing with revenue planning overtaken by product and customer profitability analysis – and by cost management – which can come rapidly from the rear. Business reappraisal becomes (probably for the first time) a major priority.

Table 3.2   *Strategic management accounting – typical priorities*

Life cycle	Revenue planning	Product profitability	Customer profitability	Cost management	Business reappraisal
Emerging	V High	Medium	Low	Low	Zero
Growth	High	Medium	Medium	Low	Low
Maturity	Medium	High	High	High	Medium
Decline	Medium	V High	V High	V High	V High
Renewal	High	High	Medium	High	High

During the 'decline' phase we now see profitability, cost management and business reappraisal all at a 'very high' priority level, whilst revenue planning hovers at 'medium'. Finally, during renewal we see a mixed picture with revenue planning reasserting its influence but balanced once again by the other four priorities.

Overall, strategic management accounting's influence is likely to peak during the 'maturity and decline phase', but still has a very strong impact during 'renewal'.

Of course one could argue that during the 'emergent' and 'growth' phases there is an equal role to play. Many of the problems during the latter phases of the life-cycle are aggravated by poor *strategic and financial weeding* of business areas at earlier stages.

3.4.2   *Life-cycle effects and financial strategy*

Market-related life-cycle effects also have implications for a company's *financial strategy* (4). Financing needs from financial strategy consists of:

> 'The matching of a company's deliberate and emergent strategies against its net funding requirements, and the requirements of external providers of funds.'

These 'net funding requirements' feature in the forecast net cash inflows from existing operations (less any planned disposals) and deliberate and emergent investment decisions. The 'requirements of external providers of finance' might include:

- a rate of return commensurate with risk
- generation of dividends versus capital growth (depending upon the nature of the shareholders)
- asset backing and/or cash flow backing – for suppliers of borrowings.

Table 3.3 now distinguishes between different stages of company growth. The table is obviously a generalisation – of which there might well be exceptions.

A few points require emphasising from Table 3.3. First, in the emerging phase, gearing might be low where a company is simply

Table 3.3   *Financial strategy and life-cycle effects*

Life cycle	Investment requirement	Cost of capital	Gearing*	Retained earnings as a finance source	Dividend policy
Emerging	Very high	Very high	Low-High	Low	No dividends
Growth	Very high	Low-medium	Low-medium	Medium	Low dividends
Maturity	Low-medium	Medium	Medium	High	High dividends
Decline	Possibly negative	Medium-high	Medium-high	High	Special dividends (capital buy-back)
Renewal	Low-medium	Medium	Medium-high	High	Medium dividends

*Gearing here is defined simply as $\dfrac{\text{longer-term debt}}{\text{total shareholders' funds}}$

unable to obtain significant borrowings – as loans. Or, it may be high because it has secured venture capital. However, much of this funding may be in effect quasi-capital (for instance, where loans can be converted to shares) requiring a high return because of the high business risk. Hence the cost of capital will be invariably high. This marries with the high importance of focusing on planning growth in revenues and product profitability that we saw in our earlier Table 3.2

Second, in the growth phase the cost of capital may be substantially lower, as the business has become established and also because investors perceive it to be an attractive venture to invest in. Once again, there is a high importance here of revenue planning, and now of both product and customer profitability during this phase, as per Table 3.2.

Third, in the maturity and decline phases, investment requirements decline, dividends rise as a proportion of earnings and there may even be special dividends declared (in effect capital repaid). This reduces the capital base and thus helps improve return on capital. There is increasing pressure to achieve a better rate of return in these phases through better product and customer profitability and cost management and business appraisal (see our earlier Table 3.2). For instance, the utility sector in the UK has seen a large amount of capital handed back to shareholders on this basis in the mid-1990s.

Life-cycle phases are not as easily separated out as our earlier typology (Table 3.3) suggests. For example, in the life insurance industry it is not at all obvious whether telephone sales channels is a 'renewal' of the existing market, or the 'emergence' of a new market.

The fact that market development has been partially triggered in the UK by new entrants to the industry (like Marks & Spencer, the retailer, and Virgin, the leisure and services group) argues for it being classed as 'emerging'. But the entry by existing players into the market following these moves suggests it is more of a 'renewal'.

Over the product/market life-cycle the bases for competing successfully will change considerably. Those changes underpin some of the key shifts in SMA priorities which we have just explained (for example, from expansion to cost reduction, and to product/service differentiation).

Even where competitors only maintain their existing competitive mix relative to customer expectations and to new technology, this alone will shift underlying competitive advantage; some competitors will innovate more appropriately and more vigorously than others.

3.5 *The impact of competitive advantage on the value drivers*

Having considered life-cycle effects, let us look more closely at the impact of changes over time on competitive advantages and their impact on the value drivers. (This reflects the 'Positioning' box in Figure 8.2 of *Exploring Corporate Strategy*.)

Changes in competitive advantage are also driven by several other factors, particularly:

- the impact of management's deliberate and emergent strategies
- the strategic intent of different competitors in the ongoing battle for market share, and for share of particular market niches
- the cumulative effects of particular combinations of competitive advantage over time. (Typically there is a lag between offering superior customer values, and this then generating increased market share, economies of scale and improvement in brand reputation.)
- the impact of changes in competitive advantage over time is explored in the following case study which deals with the UK supermarket industry.

Case study 3.1   *The impact of competitive dynamics on the supermarket industry*

The UK supermarket industry has seen a major change in the relative competitive positions of its key players between the late 1980s and the mid/late 1990s. This case shows graphically how changes in relative competitive position have a direct impact on value drivers.

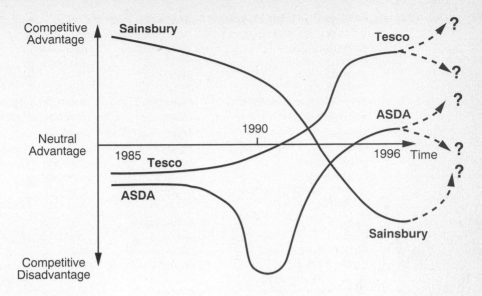

Figure 3.2   *Competitive advantage over time – the case of the UK supermarket industry*

Figure 3.2 estimates changes in competitive advantage within the UK supermarket industry over the 12-year period 1985 to 1996.

The main criteria used for determining competitive advantage of three major players: Sainsbury, Tesco, and Asda are:

- brand (increasing in importance over time)
- market share and geographic concentration (high importance throughout)
- product range, quality and relative value for money (again of high importance)
- innovation, management energy and clarity of purpose (increasing in importance over this period)
- customer service (moving from relatively low to relatively high importance).

The basis of our judgements on the industry are depicted in Table 3.4 overleaf. This table exposes our own judgements so that readers can make adjustments as they see fit. Some supermarket industry commentators may, for example, query whether Sainsbury was, in 1996, fairly characterised as being 'competitively weak'. But Sainsbury's fight-back in early 1996 through lowering prices may be symptomatic of this very weakness. Also, one might be surprised at the rapid rise of Tesco's competitive advantage between 1993 and 1996. Why, it could be asked, did this improvement not feed through quicker into improved profitability (especially as Tesco's results

Table 3.4   *Competitive advantage – our underlying assumptions*

Sainsbury	1985–1990	1991–96
Brand	Strong	Average
Market share	Strong	Strong – Average
Product value	Strong	Average
Innovation and purpose	Average	Average – Weaker
Customer service	Strong	Average – Weaker
Tesco	**1985–1990**	**1991–96**
Brand	Weaker	Average – Strong
Market share	Average	Average – Strong
Product value	Weaker	Average
Innovation and purpose	Average	Strong
Customer service	Average	Average – Strong
Asda	**1985–1990**	**1991–96**
Brand	Average	Weak - Average
Market share	Weaker	Weak
Product value	Average	Average – Strong
Innovation and purpose	Average	Weaker – Strong
Customer service	Average	Average

weakened in 1994)? But this is as a result of the lag between the time when improvements in competitive advantage occur and these improvements being harvested in superior financial performance. A two-year lag between improving competitive advantage and improving financial performance is quite common.

Ultimately, the dynamics of competitive advantage did have a very real impact on relative profitability in the industry. In spring 1997, Tesco overtook Sainsbury not only in profitability but also (for the first time) in market capitalisation.

In Table 3.4 we are talking about relatively fine differences in competitive advantage in terms of brand, market share and product value for money. But fine differences can have a significant effect over time. Also, although differences in innovation and purpose and in customer service may not be as tangible and (arguably) of slightly less importance, it is precisely here where some very big differences in eventual financial effect can be felt. As a final note it should be pointed out that by 1996 the industry had become very sophisticated – so to be characterised as 'not the strongest' should not be seen as a particularly negative criticism, especially in comparison with other industries.

Taking those specific competitive advantages, we can now relate these directly to their financial impact (see Table 3.5). This demonstrates the direct linkage between competitive advantage and the resultant financial impact. This, once again, emphasises the need to marry the strategic and financial assessment of a business within strategic management accounting.

Case study 3.1

Table 3.5 The impact of competitive advantage on the value drivers

Competitive Advantage	Value Drivers				
	Sales volumes	**Prices**	**Discounting avoided**	**Margin generation**	**Cost base**
Brand	Increased volume	Higher prices	Avoids discounting	Facilitates new products	No comment
Market share	Increased volume	May require lower prices	May require discounting	May improve (or not)	Improves economies of scale
Product value for money	Increased volume	Restricts prices	Avoids discounting	No comment	May push costs up
Innovation	Fewer increases in volume (existing and new businesses)	May enhance prices	Avoids discounting	Improved margins	Unnecessary costs avoided
Customer service	Increased volume	Probably neutral	Avoids discounting	No comment	Some extra costs but less advertising?

Case study 3.1

In understanding the impact of competitive dynamics on your own business along the lines of our Case Study 3.1, it is suggested that you should:

- identify (using the headings on the left-hand side of Table 3.5) your assumed competitive advantage (or lack of competitive advantage)

- test out your assumptions by external bench-marking (or comparison with competitors and with customer perceptions of value added)

- then, using the various columns of the value drivers (for example, sales volumes, prices, discounts avoided) identify *very specifically* where (and how) value is being lost or where more could be captured (for instance, by brand)

- then perform a 'competitive what-if' – by saying:

  'If we were to improve our competitive advantage from "X" to "Y", what might this give us through the value drivers?'

  and also:

  'What would it cost us to achieve this – in terms of investment and additional operating cost?'

- then apply the matrix in Table 3.5 by examining the contribution of each competitive advantage, row by row:

  'If we needed to make a particular improvement in how our value drivers operate (say in price increase, or discounts avoided), what additional competitive advantage would be needed to achieve?'

  and again:

  'How much extra would it cost us?'

3.6   *Identifying performance improvements*

Once one has understood the business one is in, its effects and the financial impact of changes in competitive advantage, it is now time to identify areas for improving performance.

This involves mapping out the business areas that *one is in* and relate those to the areas which it might potentially be in. This is important because the profitability of a complex business will vary considerably across its constituent parts. Managers need first to analyse what businesses they are in before, then evaluate *where* they are profitable/unprofitable, and *why*. This can be done by drawing up a series of matrices, which we illustrate selectively by plotting:

- products against market segments (for example industries served) – see Figure 3.3
- products against geographic segments
- market segments against distribution channels – see Figure 3.4
- products against distribution channels
- customer types (for example large, medium, small) against products.

Figures 3.3 and 3.4 show *how* you might begin the analysis, for example, for a retailer. The benefit of this approach is that one

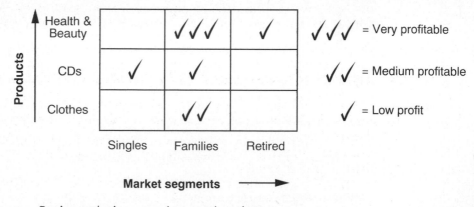

Figure 3.3   *Business design – products and markets*

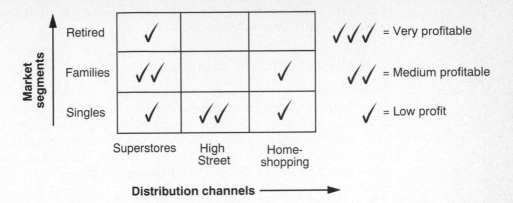

Figure 3.4   *Business design – markets and channels*

explores (visually) variations in business performance by understanding at a micro level the variation of 'what business we are in'.

Each box in these figures can then be categorised according to whether:

a) it is currently...
   • very profitable
   • of average profitability
   • of low profitability
   (or where this is a 'might do', again how this might rate in the future)

b) It should be targeted at:
   • major breakthrough (in performance)
   • continuous improvement
   • harvesting or exit.

Where this analysis threatens to become complex, you should do a Pareto-type analysis by focusing on the 20 per cent of business areas which are *most* important, or particularly interesting, or especially troublesome.

3.7 *Evaluating business and financial performance*

A more detailed level of analysis involves exposing the key drivers of profitability within selected business areas. Here the 'business area' could be a grouping of business areas with similar characteristics. For example, this might be a particular product grouping or a specific distribution channel.

At this point we focus on profitability. In order to combine strategic and financial analysis we can choose between two pictorial tools which analyse what is driving performance. These two approaches are:

- root cause analysis
- performance driver analysis.

3.7.1   Root cause (fishbone) analysis

Where a business area is under-performing, it is helpful to do a root cause analysis (sometimes known as a 'fishbone analysis' because of its shape) (5) to expose the underlying causes of the problem. In root cause analysis you begin by defining what the core symptoms of the problem are. This is then written to the far right of the page. You then brainstorm the key underlying root causes of the problem, shown as the 'bones' of the 'fishbone'.

Some managers prefer then to work backwards to a second or even more levels of detail – and on the same page. This typically ends up with a clutter of microscopic fishbones, so that only they can understand what is going on. A more preferable approach is to use a new page or flipchart when analysing each smaller fishbone. For instance, where there are six major root causes then you would have six additional pages of analysis. Obviously some root causes might be more fundamental than the others, so you might decide to be selective in your analysis. Finally, some root causes will be the 'end of the line'. An example might be, quite simply, 'senior management is not competent' (unless of course you want to query why that is so).

Figure 3.5 now illustrates a root cause (or fishbone) analysis of a particular under-performing business.

Note that this root cause surfaced both internal *and* external causes (including in the latter case attack from new sources of competition,

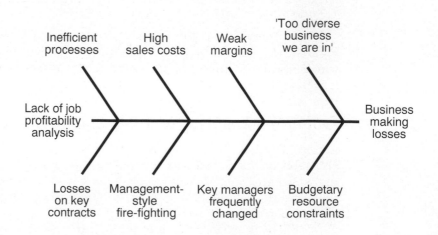

Figure 3.5   Fishbone analysis – of an under-performing business

customers getting more 'picky' and a decline in market growth rate).

Root cause analysis thus highlights the benefits of using pictorial techniques to bring to life business performance issues, rather than reliance primarily on 'gazing at the numbers'.

Root cause analysis is useful at a variety of levels:

- in understanding major corporate or business failure
- in anticipating future downturns in business and financial performance and their potential causes – both to develop preventative measures and to identify early warning signals
- at a mundane level, bringing real challenge or insight into financial variance analysis.

Root cause analysis thus provides a major focus for debate at Board level (whether corporate, divisional or business unit level), and in providing strategic management accounting reports.

The depth of thinking about performance issues can be increased dramatically by either the explicit (or implicit) use of root cause analysis. Strategic thinking encourages managers to stretch their time horizons and also to broaden thinking across functional boundaries. *Financial* analysis helps here too – giving managers a sharper idea of the consequences of problems lingering unresolved. For each problem area (or bone of the 'fishbone') is in effect *a mini business project which in turn may require decision analysis techniques (cost/benefit analysis) to identify the viability of solutions*. For instance, if we return to Figure 3.5, we might do a cost/benefit analysis of tackling the underlying performance problems as follows:

Table 3.6 A cost/benefit analysis

Problem	Option	Benefits	Costs
Too diverse a set of businesses	Exit two peripheral businesses	• Avoid annual losses £0.5m • Reduce management distraction	Incur £2.5m closure costs
Weak margins	Improve product mix and range	• Increase prices – extra revenue £0.5m • Extra volume – net margin £0.7m	Invest an extra £0.6m
High sales costs	Re-organise and re-focus sales force	• Reduce costs by £0.7m	£0.2m rationalisation costs
Inefficient processes	Re-design processes	• Reduce costs by £0.3m • Increased business flexibility	£0.2m investment

3.7.2 *Performance driver analysis*

A second way of analysing business and financial performance is to identify the key performance drivers using a tailored version of force field analysis (6) (see also *Exploring Corporate Strategy*, Chapter 11). Force field analysis was originally devised to help managers understand the enablers and constraints underpinning a particular change. In force field analysis each force (enabling or constraining) is drawn according to its perceived importance and its direction of influence.

Our application uses the same pictorial approach to identify and evaluate key performance drivers (and brakes on performance). Performance drivers here are drawn as vertical arrows and brakes are shown as downward arrows. Figure 3.6 illustrates this with reference to the perceived performance drivers of Rover cars, based on external data synthesised around late 1995.

Although this method does not purport to be an exact picture of Rover's performance drivers *it does* yield some important concerns about the medium-term attractiveness of BMW's acquisition of Rover, even if there were longer-term opportunities beyond this analysis.

Doing a force field analysis to understand the underlying drivers of financial performance can (and should) be married to quantitative analysis. In Rover's case, it would be interesting to analyse, for example, *just how much value* was being created by its four-wheel drive range, or how much value was being diluted or destroyed (annually, in millions of pounds) through Honda's transfer prices.

Figure 3.6   *Rover cars – performance (around 1995) (see also 'The BMW Acquisition of Rover Group', pages 683-90,* Exploring Corporate Strategy)

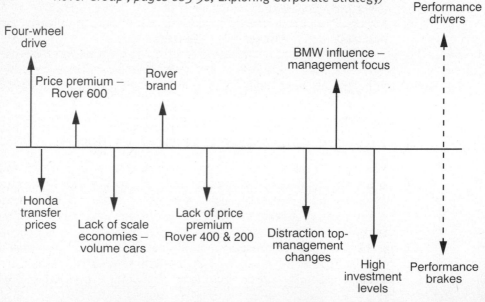

Although we cannot show the details which are of some commercial sensitivity, two key indicators suggest that our Figure 3.6 is relatively accurate:

- on German accounting principles (which are, of course, relatively conservative) Rover lost money through 1995 and 1996
- on the same accounting principles, Rover Group is *not expected to break even* before the year 2000.

The diagram in Figure 3.6 is superficially similar to our application of force field analysis to motivation/hygiene factors in Chapter 2 – Managing Strategy for Value. However performance driver analysis (Figure 3.6) also includes:

- performance drivers which are internal (for instance, the influence of BMW's management which gives Rover a sharper focus)
- negative performance drivers which push up costs (for example, lack of scale economies and high investment levels).

The performance driver approach thus incorporates internal value drivers and cost drivers, and not just the external value drivers.

Performance driver analysis can be used by managers:

- to understand what underpins an existing business unit's performance
- to understand the past performance of an acquisition target more effectively
- to target *future* performance of a business area, and to provide an aid in its business and financial planning.

Performance driver analysis can be used formally in the management team as a whole or by individual managers. But it can also be used as an intuitive tool, and does not necessarily have to be 'formally written down' to be effective.

Now that we have examined in depth the key *content issues* associated with SMA, we turn next to process issues, beginning with strategic management accounting reports, and then moving onto specific financial analysis techniques.

3.8 Strategic management accounting reports

Traditional management accounting reports are preoccupied with numerical analysis (especially of variances with some qualitative commentary). Our task here is to show how strategic management accounting reports can become much more strategic, challenging and incisive.

More mundane variance analysis may require a major re-thinking in the light of root cause analysis. Many finance departments busy themselves with a superficial level of variance analysis which

- does not really address the root causes of performance problems
- focuses instead upon operational and/or financial symptoms, and does not really look at the patterns and interdependencies which give rise to a particular malaise
- absorbs considerable time explaining away variances from a 'budget' which was originally unrealistic. This results in extensive analysis to explain why the 'wrong' performance exists when the main problem was that 'expected performance' was woefully over-optimistic.

An example of spurious variance analysis comes from a report by a Finance Director of a chain of expensive fashion stores in West London some years ago. One of his senior managers once said (of reporting to Head Office):

> 'Our Head Office in France is obsessive about us explaining the numbers. Every year it is the same. We always seem to be behind our sales targets in some months – some years it is February, other times it is May, or may be October. So what do we say to keep them happy?

> 'Sometimes we say, "Sales are down because of the very rainy weather" or "the (wealthy) Arabs haven't arrived yet this spring". But what can you do, even if it is true that the Arabs have gone somewhere else, the excuse begins to wear thin – they do have memories over there.'

This example raises the equally relevant issue (in dealing with variance analysis) of which business variables are controllable, which are uncontrollable, and which are partly controllable. Again those distinctions begin to break down when you think harder about *what you can actually do* before the event, during, and after it – and over the various times cales. For it is rare to find an event over which there is no real control over both the event itself *and* its immediate *and* knock-on consequences.

A useful approach in dealing with this is to use an 'importance-influence' grid (applied by British Telecom in considering strategic issues):

To apply this grid to performance issues, we should:

- first, identify the performance issues, evaluating these in terms of importance (see below)
- second, evaluate the degree of *perceived influence* that you have over them
- third, challenge *why* it is that you believe that you have so little perceived influence (test the perceived constraints)
- fourth, brainstorm specific opportunities for addressing these issues: can you move them North on Figure 3.7?

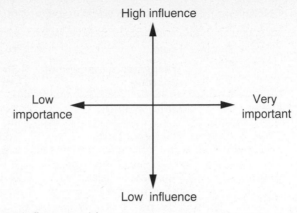

Figure 3.7   Importance–influence grid

Criteria for 'importance' could include:

- is there a high and direct impact on revenues – short and long term?
- is there a high and direct input on costs – short and long term?
- are there significant indirect benefits or costs felt in the same business or elsewhere in the company?

Returning to our theme of management reporting, budgetary processes may produce a kind of management *rigor mortis* preventing sensible strategic (and even tactical) corrective action to be taken.

Another problem that occurs is when management reporting is closely tied in with management performance targets and rewards systems – which is a natural linkage. When management rewards are very sensitive indeed to achieving ambitious performance targets then this can lead to all sorts of dysfunctional management behaviour. The effects are usually only revealed in full by corporate failures coinciding with the onset of a recession.

The big opportunity here is thus to transform internal business and financial reporting from its traditional reactive focus to give it a much more tenacious bite, as illustrated in Table 3.7 overleaf.

Before we practise some of these analysis techniques, it is now opportune to examine where (and how) some of the more specific techniques of management accounting fit in. What we are *not* suggesting is that these techniques are displaced but that they should be deployed in a more incisive manner. Also, they should be linked into *competitive* analysis.

Table 3.7   Contrasting traditional and strategic management accounting reporting

	From **Traditional management reporting**	To **Strategic management accounting reporting**
Focus	Mainly internal	External *and* internal
Time horizons	The recent past	Longer-term trends, discontinuities and *the future*
Depth	Superficial – discussing the symptoms	Driving down to the root causes
Management response	Diffuse and slow	Concentrated, selective, decisive
Presentation	Number driven	Issue and action driven with the numbers following on

3.9   Break-even, contribution and value analysis

As this chapter focuses more on the *strategic* aspects of management accounting, we have not yet mentioned some of the more traditional techniques. These also have a place in Strategic Management Accounting – this section therefore focuses on two particularly useful techniques which need to be linked with value analysis, namely:

- break-even analysis (see *Exploring Corporate Strategy,* Section 8.4.1)
- contribution analysis.

3.9.1   Break-even analysis

Break-even analysis helps managers to anticipate the activity threshold level at which a business (or a specific product) begins to make money. Generally, break-even analysis presumes a basic level of 'fixed costs'. It also presumes that the extra margin between sales revenue and variable cost is a relative constant. This difference between incremental sales revenue and variable cost is sometimes known as 'contribution'.

Fixed costs

Mathematically, the break-even point is the contribution percentage. This is because of the need for the variable contribution to cover fixed costs. For example, if there are fixed costs of £1,000 and the variable costs were 50 per cent of revenue (and the contribution percentage is then 100 – 50 per cent, a break-even point is reached at *double* the level of fixed costs. At this point sales are £2,000, giving a contribution of £1,000 (at 50 per cent) – or exactly the fixed costs of £1,000.

Break-even analysis (see Figure 3.8) can play a useful role in helping us target when activities will make money. It will also help us to estimate *what* money they will make. It can be useful in looking at trade-offs between cost structures, for example we might choose to contract out some activities, thus reducing our fixed cost base but harnessing variable costs.

However, it should be remembered that break-even analysis is somewhat limited in its value. For instance, we challenge some of its major implicit assumptions as follows:

- fixed costs are actually 'fixed': not only will they shift over time (and be semi-variable) but also in the longer term you would argue that 'no costs are fixed'.
- variable costs vary in a linear fashion: this is unlikely. They may well increase at a lower rate than turnover (due to economies of scale and experience curve effects)

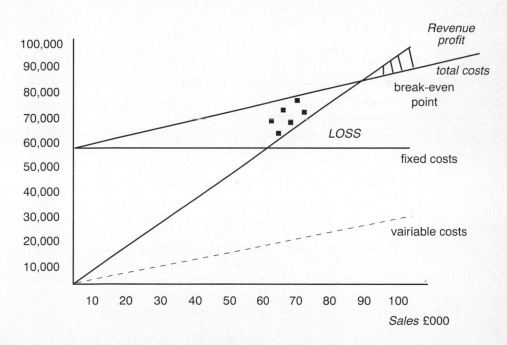

Figure 3.8   Break-even analysis – an example

- price may not remain a constant: the 'fixed price' assumption appears abstract when we consider actual competitive behaviour. Frequently sales staff may reduce price to gain market share and volume, or other discounts or other less obvious incentives (such as special payment terms) or service concessions. All of these tactics reduce revenues or increase costs, or both, raising the break-even point.

It must always be remembered that 'break-even' is just one milestone on the road to delivering shareholder value. Achieving 'break-even' does not mean that you are delivering a decent rate of return on capital. Also, as break-even is typically based on accounting-based measures, it does not represent genuine 'economic value' (see also Chapter 2).

Break-even analysis is thus often best used not at a macro-level – that is in predicting financial performance of a complex business value system. Rather it offers most potential when applied as a quick reality check against one aspect of new business development, or when reappraising a particular stream of business activity.

For example, for companies embarking on home-shopping it would be fruitful to identify the *break-even* value of the *average delivery dro*p, given a particular level of operating trading. Supposing we had for instance a home-shopping business turning over £500 million per annum, with X depots, a central administration, and so on. And suppose we had a customer base of say 300,000. Then it would be most interesting to estimate that the average value of a delivery drop needs to exceed £35, or whatever. This finding would then enable management to cross-check that the business concept was viable. Market analysis might suggest, for instance, that the value of the average drop would be constrained to £20, unless the home-shopping operation delivered merchandise from other suppliers. (All of these figures are illustrative and fictional.)

Another application of break-even analysis would be the reappraisal of existing business streams. On an incremental basis it is often easy to justify acquiring marginal revenue and avoiding shedding it. But if one were to ask the simple question:

> 'What kind of business would we have if we *only* sold product or service X, and how profitable would it be?'

We might find a disappointing picture.

In summary, break-even analysis is a core technique for understanding the point at which a business is (or is not) making an accounting profit. Break-even is only one measure and it should not be forgotten that businesses 'breaking-even' are nevertheless falling short of achieving a rate of return greater than the cost of capital. So, a break-even business is still – at least in the short term – destroying shareholder value (see Illustration 3.1 which shows the effect of break-even on an independent car repairer, 'Ronnie's Garage').

Strategy in action

illustration 3.1

Where break-even destroys shareholder value at Ronnie's Garage

At Ronnie's Garage we see how reaching a break-even still results in the destruction of shareholder value. In the longer term, it is insufficient simply to break even.

Key assumptions

	£	
Sales Revenues – currently	100,000	
Fixed Costs	40,000	
Variable Costs (per £ of sales revenue)	70%	(ie for each £1 of sales there are variable costs of 70p)
Capital required (per £10,000 of sales revenue)	4,000	
Cost of capital (and profit streams are approximate to cash flows)	13%	

Break-even calculation

Current Profit/Loss	100,000
Variable Costs 70% x £100,000	(70,000)
Fixed Costs	(40,000)
Current Loss	£(10,000)

Break-even = Fixed Costs
   divided by the contribution
   to profit of (100% – 70%)
   per each £ of sales
   Or,

$$= \frac{40,000}{30\%} = £133.333$$

3.9.2   Contribution analysis

In order to illustrate the use of contribution analysis we will use a short case study 'Business Breakthrough Consultants' (or 'BBC') – see Illustration 3.2.

Break-even analysis can also be used to break down the value

Illustration 3.1 continued

What is the return on capital?

At this break-even point, sadly, there is no return on capital. Now suppose we can increase the turnover of Ronnie's garage to £150,000 (above break-even), we have:

	£
Sales Revenues – currently	150,000
Variable Costs (70% x £150,000)	(105,000)
Fixed Costs	(40,000)
Net Profit	£ 5,000

Our capital employed is now

$$£150,000 \times \frac{(4,000)}{(10,000)} = £60,000$$

Because capital of £4,000 is required per £10,000 of additional sales, Ronnie needs to expand his range of equipment. So, simplifying our calculations by assuming that Ronnie's net profit is equivalent to net cash flow, we have:

$$\text{Ronnie's return on capital employed} = \frac{£ 5,000}{60,000}$$

or 8.3%

But this is still 4.7 per cent less than the company's cost of capital of 13 per cent, meaning that shareholder value is currently being destroyed. (Remember again our assumption that profitability is equivalent to cash flow: normally one would need to adjust for non-cash-flow elements of the profit calculation – for example, depreciation to perform this comparison.)

creation activities at a more microscopic level. For instance, in the consultancy example, we might have considerable diversity of customers and segments, some of which add considerable value and others which do not. For instance, let us look at the three big customers in our original consultancy business (which traditionally generates 60 per cent of revenue) – see Illustration 3.3.

Strategy in action

illustration 3.2
Business Breakthrough Consultants

Business Breakthrough Consultants shows how value can be diluted by extending product and service range into activities which do not add as much value as core business. Equally it demonstrates how changes in value creation in new activities can actually add value. Also it illustrates how different customers may add value or dilute value.

A small independent management consultancy (Business Breakthrough Consultants) worked principally on the basis of working (and billing) in complete days. Its focus was running strategic thinking workshops. On occasion, client demand dictated that the lead consultant worked in half-day tranches and demand was growing for this more flexible service. The company was tempted to expand this practice – in order to please both its customers and also to capture some of the extra value created.

Its pattern of trading is as follows:

Plan A

	Total revenue £
160 days fees per year at full rate £800	128,000
20 days during which half-days are delivered at £400	8,000
Total fees	136,000

(Note: it is assumed that the geographic diversity of its client base and difficult logistics invariably prohibited delivering two half-days of consulting on the same calendar day.)

As a more proactive move, the consultancy began to think about developing a senior manager counselling service. On a marginal basis (assuming nil selling time) it would be advantageous, say, to do an additional 20 half-days at a rate of £400 (or more). But did this necessarily make business sense? Supposing this counselling business took

Finally, strategic management accounting also needs to deal with the issue of cost management. This is a big issue, especially for strategic (as well as for financial) management. We therefore address this in Chapter 7 on 'Strategic Cost Management'.

Illustration 3.2 continued

off, and the core business declined, either because of external trends or because of neglect. We can then imagine a scenario of 'what would a *pure* senior manager counselling service look like, and would it be as profitable?' This would test-check the effects of 'Business Strategy Dilution' (or 'BSD' – as opposed to 'BSE'). For although the counselling business might be profitable on a marginal basis, it may nevertheless dilute *existing* business profitability or increase overall business risk (or both).

First, let us simply extrapolate the effects of the counselling business as if it were to become the whole business. Because the counselling service would be delivered in a central place, it would sometimes be possible to schedule two sessions during the same day. Potential revenues now looked as follows:

Plan B

160 plus 20 days = 180 days (of active working)

of which:

50% at 2 sessions a day = 90 x 2 x £400 = £72,000

50% at 1 session a day   = 90 x 1 x £400 = £36,000

or 270 sessions =£108,000

which is a reduction of over 20% of revenues (or a clear case of Business Strategy Dilution)!

But hold on for a moment. Consider first the *client value added* by half-day sessions – this could be considerably higher than whole days of consultancy, possibly suggesting premium pricing. Now consider how one might set about pricing this premium service, perhaps with a new mind-set. Suppose we were to offer a package of five, half-day sessions for £2,400. This £2,400 would deliver a total personal and business strategy health check (yet at a price comparable with a one-week business school programme – where one would not have exclusive one-to-one attention). Here the average fee per session becomes £480. This gives:

Plan C

Total sessions (as above) 270 x £480 = £129,600

(which is now only 4 per cent less in revenue terms than our original business plan). This shows how sensitive a financial plan is to the strategic assumptions – particularly on the market and competition underpinning it.

Illustration 3.2 continued

Obviously one can apply the wrong kind of creativity with the financial numbers to this kind of example. The strategic assumptions need to be anchored in market realism. But what it does show is that besides careful scrutiny of all new business development ideas, there is frequently ample scope for changing 'average ideas' into good, or indeed excellent, ones.

We now need to analyse the contribution levels of the various plans. Suppose we find out that the core consultancy service is expensive in terms of client acquisition, retention and in support costs. The variable costs involved are a surprising 20 per cent. By contrast, the new management counselling business is relatively easy to acquire; it is basically an order-taking operation where any additional costs are passed on to the client. Total variable costs are thus a mere five per cent. (The traditional consulting business requires costly proposal writing, telephone follow-ups, unrecovered travel costs and workshop materials.) So, comparing the two different business designs we see two quite differing levels of contribution (and ultimately profitability) as follows:

	Plan A Traditional consulting business	Plan C Counselling business (assuming £480 per session)
	£	£
Total revenues	136,000	129,600
Marginal costs	(27,200)	(6,480)
Contribution	108,800 (80%)	123,120 (95%)
Fixed costs	(10,000)	(10,000)
Net profit	98,800	113,120

Naturally, there are intermediate options between the traditional and the new business mix, and further interdependencies which need to be explored. But the above example certainly shows that emergent strategies (unless managed with some degree of deliberateness) can easily destroy or dilute value. Also it shows that using both strategic and financial analysis to *re-shape* the business can help turn a not-so-viable business idea into a much more attractive one.

Strategy in action

illustration 3.3

Business Breakthrough Consultants – contribution analysis

In any business some customers generate a higher level of contribution (sales less variable costs) than others. This may be due to differences in the difficulty of servicing them, extras which certain customers demand, or additional discounts.

	Customer A	Customer B	Customer C
Revenues	35,000	25,000	20,000
Marginal costs	7,000	6,500	3,000
Contribution	28,000	18,500	17,000
Contribution %	80	74	85

Of these three customers, A, despite being very large requires relatively intensive servicing, and the result is an average level of contribution. Customer B is a much more onerous buyer, with the result that contribution is only just 75 per cent. Smaller customer C, however is a 'star', requiring considerably less servicing. Here we would need to know a lot more about each customer as a mini-business. Does customer B exercise its bargaining factor much more effectively? Although being a blue chip name, is it really worthwhile having this business longer term? What could be done to improve the situation?

And looking at customer C, can we find more customers like C (to deliver our 'dream business')? Yes, strategic management accounting should be instrumental in getting us to address issues like this.

We also need to think about customer lifecycles – maybe customer B is costly to service principally because we are still developing its potential. Also, new and smaller accounts may cost more to service. But a test here is 'do they really have the potential to become major accounts – and over what time scale?'

Obviously in this case all of the accounts look like they break even on paper. If we assumed that the equity partner in the business required a salary of £100,000 per annum, then the current net profit of £98,800 would be very slightly below break-even. If all accounts were like customer B this would plunge the business into an effective loss. A break-even contribution rate per client is *over* 80 per cent, and nearer 85 per cent looks appropriate. How many management consultancies think about these issues explicitly when deciding to take on new business or do more work with existing clients, let alone do the calculations? One suspects, few.

Ultimately, it is always worth reflecting that it is the most important 20 per cent of current business activities which invariably generate 80 per cent of financial value (the Pareto rule). But we must also address the 20 per cent of activity that will generate *future* value say in three to five years' time. Of course these two zones of business activities will overlap, but they *will* differ in some key respects.

Case study 3.2

Virgin Direct – rejuvenating the financial services industry

Virgin Direct highlights the importance of understanding what business you are in (and not in), how value is added and the basis of competitive advantage in adding that value (see again Figure 3.1). It also illustrates the importance of life-cycle effects.

3.2.1   Introduction and background

Throughout this case study we highlight the specific techniques of *Strategic management accounting*, particularly from Sections 3.3 to 3.7. These are shown in italics.

The Virgin Direct case study illustrates many of the aspects of strategic management accounting. It highlights particularly how financial decision-making and control needs to be thoroughly strategically informed. Virgin Group was founded by Richard Branson who set up his first business over twenty years ago. Since then the Group has moved from music publishing to music retailing, into Virgin Airways, cinemas, cola, jeans, balloon flights and a range of consumer businesses. Virgin has always promised excitement to its customers – at the same time as value-for-money and high levels of service. Today Virgin Group is a complex web of private companies, Richard Branson having first floated the Group on the stock market and then off again.

Around 1993, Richard Branson, founder of Virgin Music and latterly Chairman of Virgin Airways, had a bright, new idea. According to BBC's 'The Money Programme', apparently seeking to invest some money himself, he was rather taken aback to find out how much of his hard-won investment was to go into sales commission.

Coming to the view that this was clearly a 'fat cat' industry, and one which was therefore ripe for attack, he began plotting his entry into the sector. This was achieved by redefining the way in which value is added in the industry, and the basis of competitive advantage (see again Figure 3.1).

Working backwards from what he perceived customers really wanted, he decided that their main priorities were:

- low price – delivering a value-for-money proposition
- aiming to deliver an average (as opposed to a superior) level of return
- simplicity and transparency of product design
- no real need for sophisticated financial advice
- speed of customer service
- ease of purchase

This contrasted with the most common provision of life insurance and investment products:

- often high commission-based (and large, up-front charges); those charges often being opaque (prior to recent legislation on 'disclosure')
- seeking a high level of return (but not always achieving this)
- sometimes complex and hard to understand products with proliferation of variants
- product sale must be accompanied by personal financial advice, delivered by highly incentivised sales people
- product purchase can be a tortuous process.

3.2.2   *Creating options for market entry*

Virgin's achievement was to understand how latent demand in the industry from customers seeking a convenient value-for-money proposition could be exploited. Applying the thinking behind our earlier Figures 3.3 and 3.4 *which depict matrices of products and markets, and markets and channels*, we see Virgin focusing on simple products aimed at the less sophisticated, mass market customer through a direct (telephone) channel to market. This focus gives potentially major cost advantages – some of which are shared with customers (bringing external competitive advantage), and some are taken as Virgin's intended profit margin.

Richard Branson thus set down his strategic shopping list for market entry. This included a partner who was already a well-respected player in the industry, a product which could be used to launch a brand and create a platform of market penetration, and a low-cost team operations centre to support the attack.

3.2.3   *Virgin's market entry*

So Virgin proposed to achieve a significant market presence by attacking the industry from a relatively new, *cost-leadership* direction. This was to be achieved by a telephone-sales or 'direct' operation, imitating the motor insurance company Direct Line which had attained UK market leadership through this channel.

The name for the new organisation was an easy choice – 'Virgin Direct'. This piggy-backed off Richard Branson's earlier success with the Virgin brand. This brand name was a relatively bold step, however, considering the relatively traditional culture of the industry. Investing £6,000 in an investment vehicle was hardly the same kind of a purchase decision as investing £12 in a compact disc. Branson felt he had to find a well-respected, existing player to lend credibility to his venture.

After lengthy discussions with a blue chip company, Norwich Union, Richard Branson was able to persuade its management that Virgin Direct was an opportunity not to be missed. Although this combination of youthful challenge and tradition seemed an unlikely one, Richard Branson could not have timed his approach to Norwich Union better. Norwich Union, one of the top UK insurance companies, had been put under intense competitive and financial pressure during the early 1990s. Its channels to market in the Life business were under threat and it was eager to explore new routes to market. Norwich Union was eager to team up with Virgin and no doubt hoped that some of Richard Branson's innovation would rub off.

The ingredients of Richard Branson's entry strategy were thus:

- *cost leadership*, based on a telephone-sales operation, from a low-cost operation located in Norwich

- focus on a very small number of products, initially a Personal Equity Plan (or 'PEP'). To contain costs this was supported by a 'Tracker Fund', that is a portfolio of investments whose mix reflected the stock market as a whole. This meant that the investment would not offer superior returns, but equally there would be less risk of weak returns. Managing a 'tracker' fund is much cheaper than managing a conventional fund

- to mitigate the need to advertise, Branson would capitalise on (free) publicity, particularly by soliciting media opportunities to broadcast his attack on this soft, competitive target.

We thus see Richard Branson being astute in recognising the needs of an *emerging market*. We also see how he created the *business design* of the new Virgin Direct to minimise his financial exposure (through the low-cost base). By employing a flexible labour force and having very low fixed overheads, Richard Branson was able to build into the business design a relatively low *break-even* of activity.

3.2.4 *Competitive dynamics, life-cycle effects and financial impact*

But did Branson really think through the consequent effects of his move on the market place (and thus the short- and medium-term *life-cycle* effects – see Figure 3.1)? He might easily have fallen into the trap of assuming that as his market penetration improved he would be able to become steadily more and more *profit and cash generative*.

A strategic management accounting approach might have suggested an alternative point of view. Coupled with scenario analysis (which generates a creative story-line about the future – see *Exploring Corporate Strategy*, Section 3.3.3), the following series of events could have easily been teased out:

Case study 3.2

- the level of gearing or the ratio of long-term debt to total risk capital

- the number of debtors' days outstanding, and level of stock relative to activity levels

- creditor strain – how high are *trade* creditors relative to annual value of bought-in goods and services (this needs to be based on a best estimate)?

- the cash flow statement, which highlights how cash positive or negative trading operations are, and also the extent to which this is sufficient to find investment or whether the company is sucking in vast amounts of new capital from outside.

Managers also frequently ask the question:

'What is a good (or bad) gearing ratio?'

Not surprisingly, the answer is: 'again, it depends'. Gearing is most frequently defined as:

$$\frac{\text{Longer-term borrowing}}{\text{Shareholders' funds}}$$

Relatively 'high gearing' is normally viewed as being between 50–100 per cent on the above definition. Besides balance sheet or financial gearing one also has to consider a more tangible form of gearing or 'operational gearing'. Some industries (which have lower operational gearing, ie fixed costs not so high and which are less cyclical) like non-fashion retailing, can live with a higher level of gearing than others. Property or airlines would be examples of more cyclical industries, and ones with relatively higher fixed costs, and thus operational gearing. The key point here is that one should always look at *total* gearing (even if this is approached qualitatively). Total gearing is thus given as follows:

Total gearing = Financial gearing x Operational gearing

Step 8) also entails relating the profit and loss account and the balance sheet. This is done by computing one or more measures of return on capital employed (or on 'net assets'). For ease, it is often easier to calculate the return on capital employed (or ROCE) (rather than trying to calculate both ROCE and return on net assets (or RONA)) as:

Profit before interest and tax

Net assets + long-term liabilities

For example, in the following examples we see that ROCE and RONA differ slightly:

	£m
Profit before interest and tax	15 *
Interest	4
Profit after interest and before tax	11
Tax	3
Profit after interest and tax	8
Net assets	60 (equals shareholders' funds)
Longer-term liabilities	25

To calculate ROCE take * as our defined 'profit' as follows:

$$\text{ROCE} = \frac{15}{(* \ 60 + 25)} = 17.6\%$$

(Note: A quick reminder here is that a long-standing accounting equation is that Net Assets equals Shareholders' Funds)

To calculate RONA you would need to start with profit *after* interest but *before* tax. In this example we need to take £11m as being the profit. But you would then need to divide this profit of £11m only by shareholders' funds/net assets. In this case we divide by £60m, to give a return (or RONA) of 18.3 per cent. Often ROCE is not so very different from RONA – because both pick up the same trends. The basic difference is that we are looking at returns from two different perspectives, one from purely the shareholders' perspective (ROCE), and one from the perspectives of *all* providers of capital.

Step 8 – The cash flow statement

The cash flow statement is more amenable to a high level review than it is to doing many specific ratios. It is important, for example, in examining the cash flow statement:

a) to examine whether the net cash inflow from operating activities overall *is positive*

b) to review whether net cash inflows from operating activities exceeds (or is on a par with) investing activities (unless the company is easily able to raise money from external sources of finance)

c) to compare the proportion of net cash inflow from operating activities to the cash flow from financing. Is most of the investment programme being financed from internally generated cash flow or from external sources?

A quick example

		£
Net cash inflow – operating activities		5
Interest (net) and dividends		(2)
Taxation paid		(1)
Investing activities:		
– acquisitions	(2)	
– organic	(13)	(15)
Financing – new loans		8
Decrease in cash (overall)		(5) outflow

Here, although net cash inflow from operating activities is positive, it is still small relative to the burden of financing new loans (£5m as against £8m). The net cash inflow is even smaller relative to total investing activities (£5m as against £13m). In short, this is a pretty weak cash flow position – and not just on account of one comparison, but based on several.

Step 9 – How are the financial position and prospects interrelated – what are the key business drivers?

In order to relate financial position and prospects a number of key questions still need to be posed. For instance, what overall pattern is revealed about current financial health and business performance? Is the company drifting strategically or, alternatively, has it moved aggressively into ill-thought-through ventures? Is its financial success based on (temporarily) favourable market and competitive conditions which might now be crumbling. Or, alternatively, is the company trading in a sticky and difficult market but succeeding because of statute management? To surface the business drivers invites close questioning – and from both strategic and financial perspectives.

Step 10 – What future strategic and financial prospects exist?

Further key questions which help to identify the future prospects of a company are:

a) considering its past profit growth – is this growth of profits sustainable? (Here you need to consider the underlying quality of business development, impending threats to margins, the impact of product/market life cycles and of economic cycles, and so on)

b) what do future strategies for business development reveal? (Consider statements made by the Board on the future, details of the company's capital programmes, on its innovation and market/product development plans, and so on)

c) management strengths – are they up to the task or has the business outgrown them?

Step 11 – Summarise and conclude

In our final step you should summarise the half-a-dozen key insights gleaned from your analysis. This should yield an overall prognosis, thus bringing together past financial performance, current position and future prospects – and set against a strategic context.

For example, a typical conclusion that you might reach (although hopefully not too frequently) is that:

> 'This company has embarked on an over-ambitious and unevenly-thought-out strategy for growth which is now showing early signs of failure. This is manifest in slower sales growth, lower margins and increasing competitive rivalry. The financial health of the business may rapidly be eroded and there is little sign that management realise they are entering a turnaround phase, or that they have the strength to come clean and recognise past mistakes, and to put an alternative strategy in place.'

Now that we have dealt thoroughly with the step-by-step process of strategic financial accounting, let us see it applied to the Body Shop. But before we begin the various steps we do need to say a few special words about the Body Shop's history. The following section contains a substantial case of the strategic financial accounting process.

Case study 4.1

Understanding the Body Shop through strategic financial accounting

The Body Shop is a very successful business which has increasingly come under competitive and financial pressure in the 1990s. Its Annual Report and Accounts over that period reveal a very close correlation between changes in competitive health and (following a time lag) its reported financial performance.

The Body Shop was founded in 1976 by Anita Roddick and her husband Gordon Roddick, the Body Shop began as a small shop in

Brighton, England. Since then it has grown to become an international company with retail operations across the globe (2).

The Body Shop has a unique positioning in between the volume soap and body hygiene market and the more exclusive cosmetics market. It is thus a cost leader relative to the exclusive cosmetics suppliers but has a differentiation strategy relative to the volume soap and body hygiene suppliers. Many of its products are purchased as gifts or as impulse buys.

The Body Shop's unique selling point was 'our products have not been tested on animals'. This became a motivator factor driving value which has now become much more of a hygiene factor – because other suppliers have copied the formula.

During the 1980s the Body Shop grew extremely rapidly and was highly profitable due to high margins. After the turn of the 1990s it became much harder for the Body Shop to make progress in terms of growth and profitability. This was due to:

- saturation of the UK market
- growth overseas slowing down
- competitive rivalry from new players, like Boots.

Before we analyse the Body Shop's annual results, we need to examine once again what business the Body Shop is in. For the Body Shop is, in effect, three operations in its business system:

a) sourcing and support function
b) owned retail outlets
c) franchised and 'partnership' retail outlets.

The Body Shop is a highly integrated retailer, like Laura Ashley. The Body Shop's annual report in 1994 reveals that the Body Shop Retail is primarily a *franchise operation*. Of 1,053 stores (as at 28 February 1994) 100 were 'owned by Group Companies'. The advantages of this are that the Body Shop can leverage its growth, reducing the need for external finance and management input.

The fact that the Body Shop is largely a franchise operation has a very big impact on its return/risk profile. First, it enables the company to enhance its return on assets, as its leverages off assets (capital and human) deployed by the franchisee. Second, it means that the Body Shop is dependent upon good relationships with its franchisees (a hostage to fortune). In fact in 1996 up to 31 franchisees threatened to sue the Body Shop for allegedly breaking its franchise agreements. This, it was claimed, was due to the Body Shop's plan to set up Body Shop Direct, a home-shopping arm (*Sunday Times*, 23 September).

Step 1 – Quick review of past results

We have selected a particularly interesting period of the Body Shop's history, especially from 1989 to 1994, for the purposes of our analysis. The Body Shop's annual results are now summarised in Table 4.1.

Table 4.1   *The Body Shop's financial performance*

	Years ended (selected)					
	1994 £m	1993 £m	1992 £m	1991 £m	1989 £m	1986 £m
Turnover UK	91.1	83.5	86.0	74.6	41.4	13.6
Turnover USA & international	104.3	84.8	61.4	41.0	14.0	3.8
	195.4	168.3	147.4	115.6	55.4	17.4
Profit on ordinary activities (before tax)	29.7	21.5	25.2	20.0	11.2	3.4
Percentage on turnover	15.2	12.8	17.1	17.3	20.2	19.5%

(Source: Annual Report and Accounts of the Body Shop. Note there is a gap of one year between the 1989 and 1991 results, and two years between 1986 and 1989. The 1989 and 1986 accounts are extracted from the 1992 Annual Report – to highlight the pace of growth since the 1980s.)

Several insights are evident from these figures:

- during the six-year period 1986 to 1991 the Body Shop's growth was extremely fast – a compound 46 per cent per year. Few organisations can cope with organic growth rates of this magnitude for very long. Some of this very rapid growth was due to growth in the UK, but even more impressive was the speed of the Body Shop's international development (including the USA)

- over the same 1986–91 period the Body Shop's profit (before taxation) as a percentage of turnover exceeded an impressive 20 per cent before beginning to slip back to around 17 per cent. This is considerably higher than larger retailers with a broader spread of product

- but after 1992 a significant financial setback occurred. Turnover *actually fell* in the UK, causing profits overall to drop by £3.7 million (on turnover including international up 14 per cent). Profit as a percentage of turnover fell to 12.8 per cent, before recovering to a more respectable 15.2 per cent. Part of this fall was due to a fall in gross profit margin.

Step 2 – Quick review of current and last year's profit

The operating profit for 1994 of £30.1 million is 24 per cent up (turnover being up by 16 per cent), showing a major improvement. In addition, there is a small profit on disposal of £1.1 million. Dividends are up by a conservative 18.7 per cent, given the profit increase. Staff numbers in the meantime have risen only 16 per cent.

Case study 4.1

Step 3 – Quick review of directors' report/highlights

The Directors' Report is a relatively bland account of the business, focusing mainly on policy and ethics. More interesting is the 'Business Review' (pages 8–9) and 'Financial Review' (pages 10–11).

The Business Review highlights a slower pace of shop openings with sales per unit (end-year figures) of £587,000 (previous year £578,000 – a 1.5per cent increase). This is arrived at by dividing total sales by the number of retail units. As the UK is still the largest contributor of profits, this sector needs to be watched carefully.

It is harder to get a comparable picture for unit sales outside the UK because of the very rapid pace of development.

The breakdown of operating profit is:

	1994 Op. profit as % sales	1993 Op. profit as % sales	
UK	8.1%	8.3%	Slipping
USA	8.0%	4.0%	Big improvement
International	5.7%	6.0%	Slipping
of which:			
Europe	5.2%	6.3%	Slipping
Asia	7.2%	7.5%	Slipping
Australia/ New Zealand	6.4%	4.5%	Big improvement
Americas	5.0%	5.2%	Slipping

(All figures include franchising operations)

What emerges overall is slight but noticeable margin pressure across a number of territories. The improvements in USA and Australia/New Zealand could be to do with the achievement of critical mass (based on the comment in the Body Shop report on page 10, left column, final paragraph about production volumes).

International operating profits have the potential to improve over 1995–96 as long as the Body Shop doesn't come under competitive/margin pressure. Otherwise the 'Business Review' is rather uninformative – it focuses principally upon shop openings.

Steps 4 and 5 – Profit and low ratios (and performance)

The key ratios are as follows:

	1994	**1993**
Operating profit as a % of turnover	15.4%	14.4%

	1994	1993
Gross profit as a % of turnover	54.2%	53.6%
Total operating expenses as a % of turnover	38.8%	39.2%
Selling expenses	22.0%	22.3%
Administrative expenses	16.8%	16.9%

Key comments are:

- across the board there have been very significant improvements in profit and the expense base in particular. These are likely to be due at least in part to economies of scale. The operating profit percentage is very healthy for a retailer – this also suggests it could be vulnerable to competitive attack

- page 10 in the Body Shop's report highlights that depreciation is 32 per cent higher than in the previous year

- interest expense is (currently) negligible – due to strong cash flow (note the 1994 build-up of cash (page 11) of £12.7 million).

Steps 6 and 7 – Balance sheet, cash flow and financial strength

The balance sheet reveals that total asset turnover is about the same as in 1993 (1994 – 2.02, 1993 – 2.05, dividing turnover by net assets from page 29).

Trade debtors of £24.7 million (1994) as against £22.6 million (1993) still look fairly high. Comparing these (crudely) with sales:

$$1994 \text{ days' debtors} = \frac{24.7}{195.4} \times 365 = 46 \text{ days}$$

$$1993 \text{ days' debtors} = \frac{22.6}{168.3} \times 365 = 49 \text{ days}$$

Note that because some sales are not franchise sales the denominator should be smaller, pushing up the underlying days' debtors further still.

Stocks also appear reasonably high (although these will include both manufacturer's stocks and retail stocks). Relative to cost of goods sold (a crude measure, as this will also include some labour and other costs) we have:

$$\frac{\text{Stocks}}{\text{Cost of goods sold}} \text{ x 365 in 1994} = \frac{34.6}{89.5} \text{ x 365} = 141 \text{ days}$$

$$\frac{\text{Stocks}}{\text{Cost of goods sold}} \text{ x 365 in 1993} = \frac{35.3}{78.0} \text{ x 365} = 165 \text{ days}$$

Although improving, this is a high amount. This is worrying, and invites questions about *why* stocks really need to be that high, and what would happen if there were say a 10 per cent or more over-valuation? (Note 14, page 50, highlights that most stocks are retail.)

Liquidity is good and improving, the quick ratio (or acid test) being:

1994: $\dfrac{\text{debtors + cash}}{\text{current liabilities}} = \dfrac{37.2 + 24.9}{35.6} = 1.7$

1993: $\dfrac{\text{debtors + cash}}{\text{current liabilities}} = \dfrac{33.6 + 14.0}{31.2} = 1.5$

Gearing is also becoming healthier

1994: $\dfrac{\text{long-term borrowing}}{\text{capital employed}} = \dfrac{32.4}{96.9} = 33\%$

1993: $\dfrac{\text{long-term borrowing}}{\text{capital employed}} = \dfrac{35.2}{82.2} = 43\%$

Interest cover (interest divided by profit before interest) is now 20.8 (last year 8.7). This is very good (considering the level of gearing) because of the Body Shop's buoyant profits.

Finally, cash flow is very strong, with nil external financing required in 1994 relative to a £40.3 million operating cash inflow (£38.6 million in 1993).

Overall, the Body Shop appears to be financially strong (with the proviso about debtors and stocks) *unless* there are contingent liability problems. Note 26, page 49, highlights a £3 million claim – a few others like this could be very threatening.

Now we address what are overall returns?

The Body Shop's RONA and ROCE are as follows:

	1994	**1993**
RONA:	$\dfrac{29.7}{96.9} = 30.6\%$	$\dfrac{21.5}{82.2} = 26.1\%$

1994   **1993**

$$\text{ROCE:} \quad \frac{31.2}{132.7} = 23.5\% \quad \frac{24.3}{121.7} = 20.0\%$$

The Body Shop's returns are very strong (and improving) under both measures. This is a reflection of its very high margins, which is partially dampened by its relatively intensive use of capital.

It is quite unusual to see such a divergence between RONA and ROCE (usually they are similar to within 2–3 per cent). In this case the divergence is caused by the relatively low rate of the interest charge on the Body Shop's borrowings *and* the strong profitability before interest. The additional debt in the ROCE denominator thus brings down the rate of return using ROCE. Remember that ROCE is defined as return on *total* capital employed, whereas RONA is more a measure of return on shareholders' funds – which equal net assets.

Steps 9, 10 and 11 – Past, present and future prospects – summary and conclusion

The Body Shop appears to be a classic case of a company which has created a new market and seized first-mover advantage. It has built a very strong competitive position based on a tightly organised business value system. This has generated superior value by:

- a strong, distinctive brand
- an attractive and compelling store design and meticulously presented merchandise
- high levels of customer service
- a number of 'standard-setting' products (specific cosmetics and skin creams)
- its ethical stance (products 'not tested on animals').

The attractiveness of this market was underpinned by relatively low customer buyer power (because of switching costs), initially low rivalry and a high rate of growth.

Figure 4.2 plots the trajectory of the Body Shop over the past 15 years on a General Electric (GE) or 'directional policy' grid (see Section 3.5.4 of *Exploring Corporate Strategy*). Initially moving rapidly to the enviable North-West position, it held this position during the rapid growth of the 1980s. In the 1990s it began to drift both South and East, back to a more normalised position. (So some of the disappointment with more recent results is natural – who could have expected the Body Shop to sustain its position with further innovative strategy development, and value integration?)

Clearly, the North-West positioning (in the UK) between around

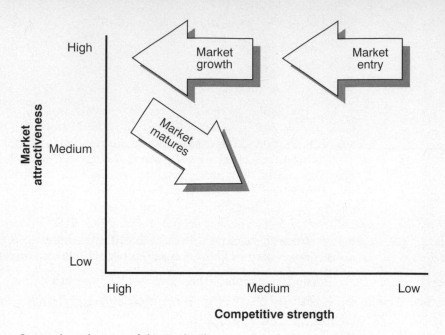

Figure 4.2   *Strategic trajectory of the Body Shop – using the General Electric or 'GE' grid*

1980-89 accounts for the Body Shop's past outstanding performance very well. Its positioning in other territories will vary considerably.

The Body Shop has clearly recovered well from the early 1990s setbacks. However, the threat of increased competitive and margin pressure and life-cycle effects is still present. The UK looks like being a most vulnerable area but it also faces strong competition in the US especially from Bath and Body Works which now has 900 outlets.

Different scenarios could be drawn out, for instance continued success on all fronts, success internationally but failure in the US, or trouble breaking out on several fronts (externally and internally) – and all at the same time.

As at 1996, the Body Shop thus continues to be a high risk investment, with risks possibly increasing as prospects of superior returns shrink. Although in 1996 half-year earnings were once again improved slightly, the volume in the UK was still flat.

By early 1997 underlying operating profits had risen 17 per cent to £38.2m but the Body Shop was forced to make a provision of £6.3m for loans made to its French franchisee. Its 287 US shops lost £3m, on static sales of £101m. Meanwhile, Asia and Pacific grew 41 per cent to £109.5m, through enthusiastic franchises. For the first time Body Shop management hinted at the possibility of applying its brand in another area – publishing (*Financial Times*, 9 May 1997).

Key lessons from the Body Shop case

A number of key lessons can be derived from the Body Shop case (per Case Study 4.1):

- when looking at any set of annual accounts and an annual report, understanding the strategic drivers of past, present and future performance is absolutely central (and not just an add-on)

- when a company is performing strongly, the General Electric grid gives a powerful 'strategic X-ray' view of many of its value drivers

- it is essential to understand the life-cycle effects at work (see, again, Chapter 4) impacting on market demand, the company's product range, its brand, and its corporate competencies

- entry barriers (and particularly the lack of them) and the level of competitive rivalry will be crucial in determining longer-term margins

- in addition, a company that 'freezes' its business value system for too long (fearing to disturb a successful formula) risks running too high a cost base, or too unwieldy and unresponsive a set of operations

- the case study suggests very important questions about the company's value drivers. For instance, what is the average spend of the customer, what drives this, and how can this be increased? (Interestingly, only 30 per cent of potential customers *actually make a purchase* when they visit a store. How can more be converted?

- the financial analysis of annual accounts highlights the effects of any strategic malaise and also helps to quantify the potential downsides of strategic drift or error – present and future.

Certainly the management of the Body Shop could now ask itself the question:

'If we were to enter the market as of 1997 from scratch, how would we enter it and where and how would we configure our business value system?'

This might well give some useful clues to a more radical value migration strategy.

4.3 Conclusion

The step-by-step strategic financial accounting process has been applied very effectively to a number of companies. For instance, in 1989 it detected the pending collapse in performance of the fashion group Burtons. (In 1991 it suggested that the financial performance of the hotel chain Queens Moat Houses could not be sustainable. In late 1995 it also anticipated the future demerger of Hanson plc.)

Strategic Financial Accounting therefore provides two powerful spotlights in past, present and future corporate performance. By combining strategic and financial analysis techniques in an integrated whole, managers, financial analysts and investors alike stand to profit much.

4.4   *Key questions*

For your own business or group, now ask:

1. What do the profit and loss ratios reveal about recent business trends and specific strengths and weaknesses in your operations?

2. How do these ratios reflect what is going on in the external, competitive environment?

3. What do the balance sheet ratios reveal about whether your assets are being used effectively and what your financial strength is?

4. How do these balance sheet ratios relate to the external market and competitive conditions? (For instance, do you have an excessively high level of debtors to accommodate the bargaining power of your customers, or are your stocks high because they do not closely fit the changing market?)

5. Is cash flow being managed within the business well or is it being dissipated, and is it adequate to support expansion programmes?

6. Does your overall analysis suggest any new strategic options for the business, for instance in terms of product/market focus, business structure or corporate mind-set?

References

(1)   Ellis J. and Williams D., *Corporate Strategy and Financial Analysis*, Pitman Publishing, 1993

(2)   See also *Exploring Corporate Strategy*, Section 5.4.1

Part 3
Strategic and financial development

In Part 3 we first examine the process for making strategic investment decisions. This begins with delivering the project, generating options, targeting and collecting data and then analysing the most critical assumptions. We also see how the problems of intangibles and interdependencies can be dealt with – before bringing this together in a business case.

We use Dyson Appliances (an entrant into the carpet cleaning market – and possibly into other markets too) to illustrate how a strategic investment decision can add value – and also for how to compile a business case.

Chapter 6 then explores the process for managing acquisitions. We begin with setting objectives for acquisitions. We explore the different ways in which acquisitions can add (and destroy) value. The imperative for having clear acquisition criteria is then underlined before we move onto considering the pitfalls (and opportunities) within the deal process – both for the buyer and the seller.

Chapter 6 also highlights the chances of under-estimating the 'iceberg' of past acquisition investment. Finally, we take readers through a long, complex and fascinating acquisition case study – of Granada and Forte.

Chapter 7 explores our final process for strategic and financial development – Strategic Cost Management (or 'SCM'). SCM integrates strategic, financial operations and organisational perspectives within a single process. We take readers through the definition of SCM issues, their diagnosis, and then onto creating challenging options. Finally, we look at evaluation and planning – and implementation. SCM is illustrated by the British Airways case.

5 Strategic investment decisions

5.1 Introduction

It is a weakness of modern management that investment decision-making is shrouded in so much unnecessary mystery. Because typically investment decisions have relatively long time scales, inevitably they are subject to the compounding effects of uncertainty.

It is frequently at the level of the specific strategic (investment) decision that the biggest opportunity occurs to integrate strategic and financial analysis. Although ongoing business planning is important too, business planning has to be set in the context of the previous strategic investment commitments already made.

Figure 5.1 now shows how strategic decisions, investment and business planning interrelate as a management process. Figure 5.1

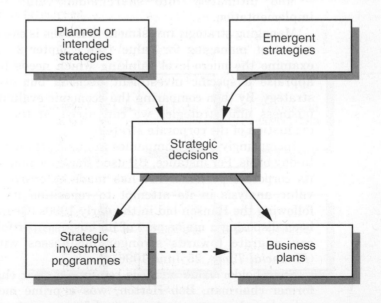

Figure 5.1 Integrating strategic decisions, investment and business planning

- **targeting and collecting data:** target data required having done a first-cut review of the kind of external and internal assumptions which will need to be made about key value drivers
- **assumptions:** collect and evaluate data through formulating the external and internal assumptions. Test these assumptions and re-visit the key options and work-up contingency plans
- **business case:** present the business case and, where feasible, refine the programme to add more value at less cost and at lowest risk
- **controls:** translate the business case into monitoring measures and controls.

5.3   *Stages in evaluating strategic investment decisions*

In this section we go through each one of the stages in the earlier strategic investment decision process, as follows.

5.3.1   *Definition*

First, if we examine the definition of the decision (or programme) more clearly we soon realise there are many problems in defining the unit of analysis. Is it a particular strategic development project or a more broadly-based programme? Where there are many and complex interdependencies it is frequently easier and better to evaluate the financials at the level of a set of projects ('the strategic project set') (see Figure 5.3).

For example, following on from the illustration in Section 3.5, if we look at the example of investing in a fleet of supermarket trolleys, one should ask:

'What is the most appropriate unit of analysis of the investment project, or programme?'

Although the costs of a new trolley fleet could be quantified, the benefits might be less tangible, for many of these benefits relate to customer value. The effectiveness of a supermarket trolley *is* of importance – from a customer perspective. This importance is part of the 'total service' effect – in combination with other programmes including:

- the level of staff service and friendliness to customers generally
- the provision of other physical conveniences – to support the shopping experience (including creche, cafe and hygiene facilities).

So it would be inappropriate to consider the investment in supermarket trolleys in relative isolation. This total customer service package is thus the strategic project set.

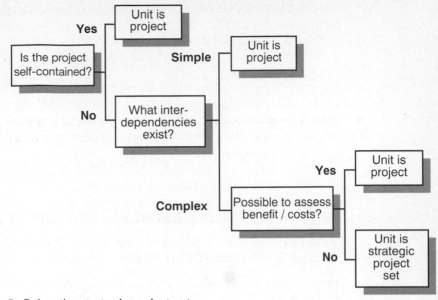

Figure 5.3   Defining the strategic project set

One of the biggest traps in analysing strategic investment decisions is therefore to analyse projects at an inappropriate level. Figure 5.3 suggests that you first need to question whether the project is self-contained or not. Only if it is self-contained can you – at that point – determine that it should be analysed as a distinct project.

Next, you need to ask whether there are many interdependencies, and if so are these simple (thus enabling them to be analysed as a discrete project) or are they complex? If they are complex then the final question is 'Is it easy to do a cost/benefit analysis of them?' (See also *Exploring Corporate Strategy*, Section 8.3.1.) If it is not easy, then you should not analyse this as a separate project. Instead, you should analyse it amongst part of a higher level set of projects, or the *strategic project set*.

For instance, investment by a major brewery in a strategic change programme for its senior and middle managers was seen as being a discrete 'training' or skills-based investment. But when this was examined more closely, the main value of the programme was realised through a number of strategic changes in the business being subsequently led by those managers rather than merely handed over to management consultants, such as business restructuring.

5.3.2   Options for defining the project

There are invariably many different options for defining a strategic investment project, for instance:

- should the strategic objective be achieved through organic or through acquisitive activity?
- is it more appropriate to move very quickly or slowly?
- is it worthwhile piloting development prior to making a bigger commitment (usually it is)?
- should commitment be delayed until there is a sufficiently strong implementation capability, enough resource, and the right timing?
- should a number of product/market routes be pursued simultaneously (thus perhaps spreading resources too thinly), or should one major project be progressed at a time?
- can the project's key objectives be fulfilled at lower cost or with more flexibility through an alternative option?
- if we go ahead with this particular project, what other options (present and future) does this decision foreclose?

5.3.3   *Targeting and collecting data*

Once you have identified one or more options you should then identify the cash flow impact of the investment. For instance, in Illustration 5.1 (overleaf), investment in a new product might have the following impact on cash flows (assuming a product life of three years).

5.3.4   *Evaluating the assumptions*

Defining the assumptions requires considerable debate and challenge to provide a realistic basis for a business case. For example, if we go back to the new product investment decision in Section 5.3.1, we might identify a number of key assumed/value drivers, for instance:

- the new product adds superior customer value, enabling it to:
  –sustain volumes (in existing customers)
  –increase margins (slightly)
- also, this enables new customers to be penetrated
- the level of competitive rivalry is a value driver (as this might increase or reduce prices).

  Cost drivers also include:

- the unit costs might be influenced by levels of activity through economies of scale
- the cost of new product development is a key cost driver.

Frequently, investment cases omit or take-for-granted many of the implicit external assumptions. Although incremental sales volumes, prices and margins are invariably spelt out, less thoroughly examined are things like competitive behaviour and key elements of the customer's business value system.

Questions which help to test out the *external* assumptions for a

Illustration 5.1 continued

strategic investment project are therefore as follows, under the headings of:

- the competitive environment
- customers and market trends.

These questions give managers a checklist for appraising any kind of investment decision.

Questions on the competitive environment include:

1. What competitive assumptions are implied by projected volumes, prices and margins, and how do these change over the life-cycle?
2. How might specific competitors be either addressing the same opportunity already or might they be able to respond quickly to your move?

Questions on customers and market trends include:

1. How do customers perceive the value of any end product or service upon which the opportunity depends? (Consider perceived image, cost savings, risk levels.)
2. How important is this value creation within the customer's own business value system, and what interdependencies is this contingent upon?
3. How powerful are customers relative to the company and to what extent is the additional value created harvested by customers versus the company?

In addition you need to consider the life-cycle effects which we described in our previous chapter on strategic management accounting. This chapter also covers the need to break down the various segments of the market, its distribution channels and sales by major type of customer in formulating your assumptions.

To test the *internal* assumptions underpinning a strategic investment decision it is now suggested that the following questions are asked. These deal with investment, costs and implementation assumptions.

Investment-linked assumptions include:

1. What capacity levels are assumed and are these assessed in relation to the operating cycle over a whole annual period?
2. What unforeseen areas of investment may be required either of a future or indirect nature (for example expansion of office space) not currently included in 'incremental' cashflows?
3. What investment is implicitly required by customers (either in capital or non-capital) and what is the perceived return/risk to them, and over what timescales? (Consider here the investment required to switch sources of supply.)
4. What hurdle rate of return is appropriate for this project?

Figure 5.5). The uncertainty tunnel is depicted as a tunnel bounded by constraints on what is possible within an industry (or business).

Here change is explored by looking at the precursors of the change (what has gone on before and why – and what is the build-up leading to a discontinuity). Secondly, managers analyse these factors either amplifying or dampening a particular change. What is their relative balance? Are these amplifiers cumulative? Are there specific dampeners which will delay or prevent a change?

Following this analysis we then examine the immediate versus the longer-term consequences of change, perhaps discriminating between first, second and third order consequences. This enables the effect of customer and company learning, and competitor responses to be brought into the equation.

There may, of course, not be a single 'uncertainty tunnel' but more than one. For instance, if a new type of technology begins to percolate through the larger computer system market, it may go through two phases of uncertainty:

1. initial take-up by companies and application ('Future 1')
2. Learning about how the new systems add, dilute, or destroy value, and additional investment to develop new computer platforms ('Future 2').

In this example, the 'uncertainty tunnel' would allow managers to build up shared mental maps of how value would be created, and what is the financial potential of particular investment programmes in new types of products. Note here the need to distinguish between not just a single future but a number of futures.

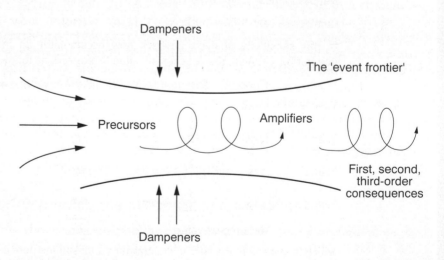

Figure 5.5   The uncertainty tunnel

5.3.7   *Exploring the 'do-nothing' or base case*

Before we leave the topic of assumptions we also need to explore the 'do-nothing' or base case option (6).

The base case is what might happen without the investment decision. Traditional financial theory teaches us to evaluate incremental cashflows – 'incremental' meaning the difference between net cashflows both with and without the investment project.

A major problem with the base case is that of predicting the rate or pace of decline. This is inherently difficult to predict. Some managers may then try to shield financially suspect projects behind the argument that unless the project is implemented, the strategic and financial health of the business will be irreparably damaged. See Figure 5.6 for a classic illustration of a declining base case.

The important thing to remember with the base case is that you need to spend almost as much time thinking about the world in which one does not do the investment as the world in which one does.

5.3.8   *Intangibles and interdependencies*

Dealing first with intangibles, strategic investment decisions add value only insofar as they are part of the business value system. Interdependencies thus need to be explored because they are essential in understanding how the business operates as a total competitive and financial system.

Interdependencies exist in a variety of forms. Some interdependencies are external and reflect the impact of one external assumption on one another. For example, a resurgence of economic

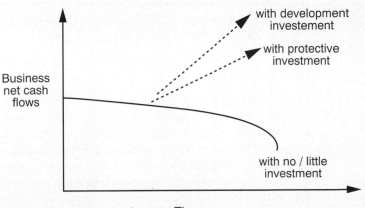

Figure 5.6   The effects of the declining base case

growth may increase the size of a particular market and also attract in new entrants.

Many of the internal assumptions depend upon external variables, giving rise to even more interdependencies. (For instance, competitive rivalry may lead to a high incidence of price discounting and thus to lower margins.)

But many of the more interesting interdependencies are those within the architecture of the business strategy itself. For instance, one product may benefit or suffer due to the introduction of a new product. FMCG companies realise this and also supermarket chains opening superstores – these companies are acutely aware of cannibalisation effects. But this is not so commonly appreciated in many other industries.

The analysis of interdependencies should follow on from the analysis and testing of the external and internal assumptions. Where the decision process is of a less formal nature, analysing interdependencies should be integral with the evaluation of assumptions.

Intangibles are one of the main curses of strategic investment decisions. For many managers, intangibles have become the 'no go' zone of financial analysis. Although these are areas of value extremely difficult to quantify in financial terms (and perhaps impossible to quantify with precision), there are invariably ways of defining intangibles better. This can be done by looking at the project from different perspectives:

- competitive: impact on customer perceptions of value or in measurable improvement *vis-à-vis* competitors

- operational: performance improvement or flexibility of operations

- organisational: impact on morale and, indirectly, on motivation
- opportunity generation: the opportunity which might be opened up or explored as a result of the investment project.

The first step with intangibles is to ask 'why is the value thought to be of an intangible nature?' This may be because:

- the benefit accrues to the customer rather than directly to the company. However, there may also be indirect benefits to the company via reducing the customer switching its source of supply, or through increased orders (and volume), or through increased prices, or through protection against discounts. For example, when Hewlett Packard tried to appraise the value of attaining a particular quality award, it found that most of the value came relatively indirectly and could not be harvested in a simple or direct way

- the benefit may be of a future and essentially contingent nature. This may be contingent because a future state of the world is required to crystallise a market – this may require alignment of a credible product offering, customers recognising the need exists, and potential demand actually crystallising. Even in this situation, your particular company needs to be credible as a supplier to generate value

- the benefit accrues via a number of internal interdependencies with other areas of the business, or these may occur because the investment project is essentially part of the 'business' infrastructure

- the benefit comes due to the project being essentially protective or defensive in nature.

A process for dealing with intangibles is therefore:

- to identify why the value is of an intangible nature

- to seek possible alternative measures to help target and provide indicators of alternative measures to those of purely financial value (see Table 5.1 overleaf). (Once again, the use of customer motivator factors and hygiene factors met – see Chapter 2 – will help in teasing out what value can be created and harvested.)

- through management consensus, to compare what value managers are prepared to put on the intangible.

An example of managing intangibles can be drawn from ICI's expansion into the international seeds business in the 1980s and 1990s. A number of acquisitions of family-owned seeds businesses were made, with ICI paying significant sums for 'goodwill'. These businesses were held at the time to have considerable intangible value, particularly:

- through providing the platform to exploit new breakthroughs in genetic technology (but what was the likelihood of this breakthrough, how would ICI capture its value in the market place – using these companies, and for how long?)

- by achieving operational synergies with the other newly acquired companies (but *who* would harvest these synergies, *how* and *when*?)

In the event, these intangibles proved elusive for ICI, the moral being: do not hide behind the difficulties of evaluating the intangibles.

We now explore a company which has been conspicuously successful in harvesting the value of its investment decisions. The company in question is Dyson, a privately owned but rapidly expanding supplier of household carpet cleaning machines. Dyson's innovative product is a distinctive, innovative and premium-priced suction machine for domestic use. The following case study demonstrates the inextricable linkages between strategy and value when making any kind of major

Table 5.1   Types of intangibles and possible measures

Types of intangibles	Related to other appraisal problems	Possible focus for measurement
Product image	Customer value	Customer views of product
Reduced customer product and service	Customer value	Customer views of costs and risks
Customer loyalty	Customer value	Estimated revenue and likelihood of switching
Protection of business	Protective investment	Monitoring incidence of existing loss of business
Spin-off opportunity	Contingent value and interdependency	Specify conditions under which opportunity arises and is harvested
Flexibility	External and internal interdependency	Specify conditions under which flexibility will add value
Cost savings elsewhere	Internal interdependency	Before and after measurement of cost drivers and of impact
Alignment of external and internal factors	External and internal interdependency	Specification of conditions under which alignment may occur and probable value

business investment. Following the case study we then describe how to set about creating a business case for a strategic investment decision before applying this to a new opportunity facing Dyson.

Following on from the Dyson case study, Dyson's planned strategy enabled him to achieve a number of competitive, operational and financial benefits from his investment simultaneously. These are shown in Figure 5.7.

This shows the kind of picture which managers should draw (or at least visualise) for every major, strategic investment decision. This model is *at least as important* as doing the financial numbers themselves. Indeed, it provides a real understanding of the basis for any positive 'NPV' rather than assuming that if the numbers 'look good' then the investment must be sound.

Following the Dyson case, let us now examine what should be in a business case before applying this process to a Dyson opportunity ourselves.

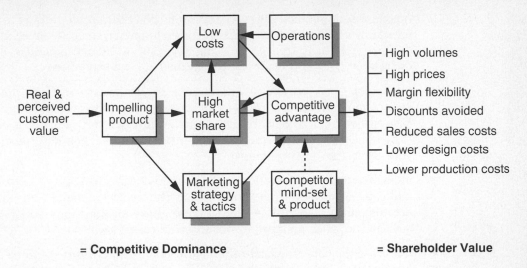

Figure 5.7 *Dyson's strategic investment decision*

5.3.9 The Dyson breakthrough – and defining the business case

When someone says the words 'business case', managers often think of a weighty, detailed document with lots of hard facts and financial numbers.

But the real point of a business case is to gain more clarity about the objectives of the project, its implications for the business and particularly to expose and test the key assumptions which drive value. This can be achieved in a very succinct way, by, for example restricting the business case to a maximum of eight pages, as noted below (often fewer will suffice):

Format for a business case

- executive summary (1 page)
- project definition, objectives and scope (1 page)
- how the project adds value (new opportunity, tangible synergy, defensive or protective value) (1 page)
- key external and internal assumptions (with an evaluation of importance and uncertainty) (3 pages)
- implementation issues (1 page)
- summary financials (1 page).

This brings the total length to eight pages plus detailed appendices containing technical details, detailed financial and non-financial measures and milestones, detailed financial sensitivities, detailed resource requirements – possibly another seven pages. This brings a typical case to just 15 pages. (Later on in this chapter we illustrate the format of a business case with reference to our Dyson case study.)

Some practical tips on putting together a robust business case include:

- involve a good spread of managers in project definition, option generation and data collection in a targeted way. This will ensure your assumptions get a good reality check, and that you identify a good range of options, implementation constraints, and begin to position your project for endorsement

- be disciplined in data collection: only collect data which will help you make the critical assumptions which the project depends on. (This actually means spending less time on those assumptions which are less critical, such as more minor internal costs)

- integrate the data in a preliminary workshop – to evaluate options and assumptions in a creative way. (Do not lose focus in a series of meetings spread over time.)

- take the point of view of other stakeholders in the organisation. Consider which assumptions are *most important to them* and where will their judgements differ from yours, and why. Experiment here with the 'out-of-body' experience – imagine you actually are those stakeholders – what attracts you towards or repels you away from the project?

- do not try to obscure or conceal the project's downsides. An astute review panel will quickly identify issues which you have glossed over. Your 'out-of-body' simulation will equip you to have a balanced debate on the merits of the project.

Business cases will only add value therefore if:

- they are clear, succinct, and written in a jargon-free style

- they expose the most important and uncertain assumptions, and also address these both in the sensitivity analysis and via contingency planning

- they do not fall into the trap of seeing the financial numbers as absolute measures of value, but use these creatively. For example, in dealing with fewer tangibles it may be fruitful to put an illustrative value on 'what these might be worth', so that a more balanced, overall appraisal of the project can be achieved.

We have argued throughout for the need to understand the key value drivers and to expose and challenge the key assumptions *before* undertaking the sensitivity analysis (as we saw in the new product launch in Illustration 5.2). 'Better practice' means doing very rigorous testing of those key variables which are likely to be most uncertain and most important.

It is only by working this way around that true sensitivity analysis is performed, otherwise all you end up with is 'insensitivity analysis' – playing with the assumption set to get the right answer, that is, a positive net present value, (or 'NPV') (which in this case means no more than 'numbers prevent vision').

Finally, an important issue is how to deal with the terminal value. This is the value which is put on the cash plans at the end of the time horizon of the projections. With slow payback decisions the terminal value can amount to between 40 per cent and 50 per cent of NPV. Yet terminal value may be subject to minimal, strategic and financial scrutiny. Invariably, terminal values can be proved more effectively using a quick competitive and financial scenario which, although broad-brush, checks that the assumptions make *prima facie* sense.

Having looked at the practical issues of formulating a business case, let us look at how James Dyson's investment to enter the carpet cleaning market added value. The following case is a prelude to considering a hypothetical business case for Dyson to enter the washing machine market.

Case study 5.1

Dyson appliances – a strategic investment breakthrough

Dyson's breakthrough in the carpet cleaning business demonstrates the importance of aligning all critical areas of the business value system both internally and externally to deliver shareholder value.

5.1.1 From inventor to entrepreneur

In the mid-1990s, James Dyson, founding Chairman of Dyson, decided to take on other players in the domestic carpet cleaning industry with a rather different proposition. He decided to discard the taken-for-granted assumption that such devices needed a bag. Dyson decided that – far from adding value to the customer – the bag was actually an unnecessary cost and a bother to replace. Worse, Dyson contended that the bag itself actually reduced the effective power, and thus the performance, of the carpet cleaner. Dyson's new product, a distinctively designed, yellow, expensive and bagless floor cleaner, gained market leadership in the UK carpet cleaning market.

James Dyson invented and patented a device which enabled his cleaners to do without a bag, using a very fast circling vortex of air. The dust was drawn up into a perspex tube or cylinder where it was dropped. Periodically the user would empty out this cylinder *without producing a small dust storm*. (This is because of its being packed densely as it is drawn to the side of the cylinder as the air is circulated at high speed.)

5.1.2   *Going for competitive knockout*

Now Dyson could have stopped at this point in designing his strategy but he decided not to do so. Instead, he set about achieving a compelling customer pull, and a dominant competitive advantage. Intuitively James Dyson recognised that to leapfrog over companies like Hoover and Electrolux he needed to align a *number of points of competitive leverage*. Only then could he secure a financial advantage. Each one of the points of competitive leverage procures financial value (and where this occurs the case study is italicised).

So let us now represent these points of leverage using a pictorial tool called 'wishbone analysis'. The wishbone analysis in Figure 5.8 highlights just how many points of competitive leverage Dyson focused on. It also emphasises how dependent his strategic success was on areas where he had relatively low influence (for example, on the assumption that the major industry competitors would not change their mind-set significantly).

Figure 5.8 also emphasises how Dyson did not just set about exploiting its strategy from a technology-led point of view. In particular, he experimented with marketing innovation to achieve a compelling advantage. (For instance, he offered his products at half price to electrical goods retail sales people – to encourage trial.) Figure 5.8 in its totality shows how well articulated Dyson's strategic thinking (and his strategic vision) was.

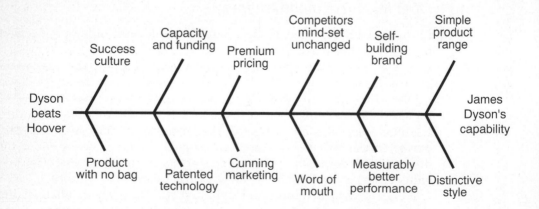

Figure 5.8   Wishbone analysis

5.1.3   Turning competitive advantage into hard cash

Interestingly, this 'wishbone' was not achieved in one fell swoop. Dyson had previously penetrated the Japanese market with a £1,000 machine. It was based on the lessons of this experience that Dyson's mid-1990s deliberate strategy, with a price of over £200, was formulated. Developing an effective 'wishbone' may thus take a number of iterations as the strategic concept is fleshed out or experimented with. *The premium price of £200 was thus a key value driver in the Dyson investment decision. This produced exceptional margins.*

The results of this strategy were spectacular. In a short period of time Dyson had achieved a major share of the market. Within two years Dyson had moved from employing fewer than 20 people initially to employing 300 (and, in 1997, standing at 560) from a purpose-built, greenfield site. *This move enabled Dyson to guarantee quality (at high volumes) thus protecting customer value, and to reduce unit costs through effective production methods and economies of scale.*

According to *The Times* (8 February, 1997), Dyson's company has now reached a turnover of more than £100 million per annum *in just three years* since the launch of its core product, enabling him to buy a £3 million country house as his new home in Christmas 1996. His margins are rumoured to be of the order of the Body Shop in the 1980s His book *Against the Odds* is a fascinating account of success. (7).

5.1.4   Creating 'built-in success'?

This wishbone analysis, which is in effect a visual representation of the strategic project set (see Section 5.3.1 and Figure 5.3), highlights a number of important lessons:

- when a strategic investment decision is targeted at creating a major strategic breakthrough it is perhaps rare to find that this is dependent on only a small number of factors. It usually involves getting a considerable number of things right, and having favourable external circumstances and good timing which results in value generation

- where strategic success proves elusive, this may well be because of just one, two or possibly three factors which either were not well-aligned, or which were completely unaligned. Dyson's success began by working backwards from customer value (and value to the distribution channel) and by engineering his entire operations to deliver that value

- some of these factors may be to do with the *competitive strategy*, and some of its implementation. (The wishbone analysis thus helps us focus on implementation as well as *positioning* issues. Note particularly how we have defined James Dyson's own capability as the 'backbone' of the wishbone

- the various bones on the fishbone are interdependent. When they co-exist, additional value is created. For instance, the bottom bones of the fishbone deliver a natural and impelling demand for the product. The top bones both help to lower its costs, increase its price, protect that price and facilitate expansion. They are part of one large 'strategic project set' (see Section 5.3)

- taking the wishbone analysis as a whole, the various factors will differ both in their degree of *importance* and in terms of *influence levels*. This leads on to a more in-depth analysis to extend the domain of our control over the strategic vision, helping identify (and reduce) the likely implementation gap.

In Dyson's case the 'competition's mind-set is likely to remain unchanged' appeared to be both very important and something over which Dyson had low influence. Had Dyson's competitors been able to counteract directly, this might easily have destroyed value – through much reduced volumes, reduced prices, increased discounting and by also pushing up operating costs. A critical issue for Dyson was thus *how* did he encourage them to believe that by continuing to sell machines with a separate bag this offered the best route forward? Obviously, the fact that he had a strong patent protection was a useful tactic. But by encouraging a public debate on the relative merits of 'the bag' versus 'no bag' he encouraged them to dig into (and become more committed to) their existing mind-set.

If we now go back in time to the point where James Dyson evolved his own business case for expansion, we could easily do a financial plan with:

- sales revenues = sales price x volume
- variable costs
- fixed costs
- working capital and capital investment
- cash flows and an NPV.

But more importantly, the critical value drivers (which should be identified in a business case) are:

- customers' perceptions of the superior value of the Dyson product – and willingness to pay a price premium

- the company's ability to satisfy premium customer expectations throughout all of its product and service delivery

- competitors' inability to compete head-on with Dyson – or to evolve an alternative and more effective strategy

- Dyson's ability to harvest a good proportion of his product's premium price through its retail channels

- the company's ability to gain cost economies through scale and simplicity of product range.

In James Dyson's television interview (the *Money Programme*, 1995), he conspicuously *did not deny* the possibility that he was considering developing a washing machine based on his 'cyclone' technology. Let us now suppose that this is a serious opportunity for him. The following are extracts from a hypothetical business case.

5.1.5   The Dysonmatic – cleaning up the washing machine market

(A fictitious business case)

James Dyson, having successfully penetrated the carpet cleaning market now turned his attention to washing machines.

Following on from the *strategic* analysis of the Dyson opportunity, his business case for expansion should also have defined:

- prices (over time) – and dealer discounts
- sales volume (over time) – and the mix for product variants
- sales, marketing and distribution costs
- production costs
- administrative costs
- investment – both initially and during the investment in both fixed assets and working capital.

These would be translated into cash flows. Due to commercial constraints we cannot show you James Dyson's own business case.

(Any resemblance to any Dyson business strategy is purely coincidental. However, what we can do is to illustrate, with reference to a hypothetical new product, investment which Dyson might undertake.)

His summary business case is shown as follows:

Executive summary

Dyson was to set up a new division, 'Dysonmatics' to attack the washing machine market. This was intended to achieve a five per cent market share within three years and to take market share from existing competitors based upon:

- Dyson's branding

- a distinctive design (the machine would be yellow and curved, rather than a conventional box shape)

- the cyclone technology would be applied to produce a quicker, more economical wash with *total removal of dirty stains* (hence being more effective than a conventional machine)

- following Dyson's competitive strategy elsewhere, it would be premium priced retailing at £700 per unit.

Project definition, objectives and scope

The business was established separately from Dyson's core operation, but incurred a management charge for Dyson Group's administration, and research and development. Its objectives were to achieve a five per cent market share within three years, to become cash positive by the beginning of year three. It would also achieve a minimum internal rate of return over 18 per cent over the first three years and of over 20 per cent over the first five years.

Project value added

The project would generate considerable cash streams in its own right. It would also enhance Dyson's brand (both for its core business – carpet appliances, and also for new ventures elsewhere). Although a (quantified) value was not put on this brand enhancement, James Dyson's best estimate of this value was that not going ahead with Dysonmatics would be a financial 'regret' to the tune of £2 million. This value was, however, not included in the financial projections and evaluation.

Key external and internal assumptions

The market for washing machines was not itself growing significantly, but Dyson's product entry would very marginally increase total market demand. Roughly a third of sales would come from pure market expansion and two thirds from existing competition. Market growth would come from accelerating replacement of older and ineffective machines (which have not yet broken down).

The Dysonmatic would be produced in a separate plant adjacent to the Dyson site. This required some purchase of land but the main investment (of £4 million) is in a production facility.

The retail price of each machine was, initially, £700 (trade price being £400 – which allowed an attractive dealer margin). Prices would be assumed to fall slightly (net of discounts) over three years. Variable production (and other) costs were £280 per machine (again falling over time).

It was assumed that competitors would not seek to imitate the design of the product and would not imitate its (patented) technology. But after five years the product (and production line) would need replacing (having nil residual value). This was a deliberately pessimistic assumption.

A major assumption (both very important and uncertain) was the rate at which the net price – to the trade – would fall due to competitive rivalry (and product imitation) in years three to five.

Implementation issues

A new, dedicated management team would be established to ensure that the division was successful and did not dilute management resource in the core business.

Table 5.2   Summary financials – Dysonmatics

	Year 0	Year 1	Year 2	Year 3	Year 4	Year 5
Sales units		20,000	50,000	100,000	120,000	120,000
Sales price (to trade)		400	400	360	360	360
Variable costs		280	260	250	250	250
		£m	£m	£m	£m	£m
Sales revenues		8.0	20.0	36.0	43.2	43.2
Variable costs		5.6	13.0	25.0	30.0	30.0
Fixed costs		1.0	1.5	2.2	2.2	2.2
Net revenues		1.4	5.5	8.8	11.0	11.0
Working capital (15% of turnover)		(1.2)	(1.8)	(2.4)	(1.1)	—
Fixed capital	(4.0)					
Working capital released						7.7
Net cash flow	(4.0)	0.2	3.7	6.4	9.9	18.7
Discounted cash flow	(4.0)	0.2	2.6	3.7	4.7	7.5

The net present value (assuming operating revenues equate to net cash flows) for Dysonmatics would therefore be £14.7 million (applying a cost of capital of 20 per cent) *less* the present value of taxation paid of an assumed £5.1 million (35 per cent), or £9.6 million. This £9.6 million exceptional return was wholly dependent upon Dyson's assumed (sustainable) competitive advantages.

For instance, if Dyson had to drop his trade price to £320 in years 3, 4 and 5 this would have an impact of:

Year 3	Year 4	Year 5
(4.0)m	(4.8)m	(4.8)m

$$x \left(\frac{1}{(1.20)^3} \right) \quad x \left(\frac{1}{(1.20)^4} \right) \quad x \left(\frac{1}{(1.20)^5} \right)$$

$$= (2.3)m \quad = (4.8)m \quad = (1.9)m$$

or a £6.5m decline in its NPV *before taxation* from £14.7m to £8.2m.

5.4   Conclusion

Strategic investment decisions are at the very heart of strategy-making and implementation – just as the lags between strategic action and pay-off are significant. High levels of financial return typically do not occur in commodity industries; they in industries with complex *business value systems*, and in ones with complex significant entry barriers and where there is an investment in customer switching costs. These high levels of returns are also found when companies can seize an advantage through *strategic mobility* – that is, through their ability to move rapidly and decisively into new markets or to change existing ones. Once again, this strategic mobility typically requires the deployment of significant investment, but this very risk demands its own superior return.

5.5   Key questions

Key, high-level questions to ask yourself on strategic investment decisions are:

1. Do managers genuinely understand the technicalities of financial appraisal and what problems are caused when they do not?

2. Do managers have a deep and intuitive understanding of the links between the financial and the strategic appraisal? Where they do not, how robust are the resulting business cases typically?

3. Are business cases mainly a way of rubber-stamping what has already been agreed, or is a business case a genuine forum for creative and challenging debate?

References

(1)   Grundy A. N., *Corporate Strategy and Financial Decisions*, Kogan Page, 1992

(2)   Brealey R. and Myers S., *Principles of Corporate Finance*, McGraw Hill, 1984

(3)   Grundy A. N. and Ward K., (eds) *Strategic Business Finance*, Kogan Page, 1996

(4)   Mitroff I. I. and Linstone H. A., *The Unbounded Mind*, Oxford University Press, 1993

(5)   Ghemawat P., *Commitment – The Dynamic of Strategy*, The Free Press, Macmillan, New York, 1991

(6)   See *Exploring Corporate Strategy*, Chapter 7, Section 4

(7)   Dyson J., *Against the Odds*, Orion Business Books, London 1997

6

Strategy, acquisitions and value

6.1 Introduction

Acquisitions are typically a major route for strategy development (see *Exploring Corporate Strategy,* Section 7.2.3). In this chapter we show how acquisitions need to be managed with a clarity of strategic thinking in order to yield financial value.

Managing acquisitions entails a very close integration of the strategic and financial management disciplines. We have already seen (in Chapter 5) how difficult strategic investment decisions can become – due to factors like uncertainty, intangibles and interdependencies. But for acquisitions we face even greater hurdles to surmount, particularly as we may *know less* about the business value system of our target company; we may also be unable to predict with much confidence how it will interface with our own business value system.

Whilst managers' knowledge about an acquisition may thus be inferior (as compared with internal investment to develop the business), their commitment levels can be easily higher. This is because acquisitions appear to offer an accelerated path towards achieving strategic goals. Also, they are more obviously exciting to managers – both in making the acquisition and in furthering career paths.

Whilst organic investment is frequently subjected to a tough appraisal regime, acquisitions are sometimes given a strategic, financial and political head start.

First, a *strategic head start* arises usually because acquisitions are typically seen as aggressive moves which reposition the business or group almost immediately. Acquisitions are labelled strategic because they are bold but not necessarily because of their carefully thought through logic.

Second, a *financial head start* may arise because acquisitions may not be exposed to the same financial rigours as internal investment decisions. Managers may frequently focus on 'the multiple of current

In addition to the value segmentation over the phases of the acquisition – V1, V2 and V3 – we also need to analyse the different ways in which the business strategy itself adds value. One useful approach is to distinguish between:

- **enhancing and protective value:** the value which can be added either by strengthening the acquired business's current competitive position and scope; and the value to the acquirer of a defensive nature – for example, in avoiding loss of economies of scale

- **opportunity value:** the value of the opportunity stream inherent in both the acquired company's markets and its existing platform. This value can come from possible new products, services, network channels or technologies, or simply through fast market growth generally

- **synergistic value:** the value of bringing together particular activities within the business value systems

- **sweat value:** the value released by pure reduction of costs or assets in the acquired company, or the potential disposal of whole businesses.

Figure 6.2 shows how this value segmentation can be pictured in diagrammatic form. It shows how Lloyds Bank's acquisition of Cheltenham and Gloucester Building Society in the UK appeared (based on press commentary) to be viewed. Figure 6.2 is also useful for controlling and learning from acquisitions during integration. Did the

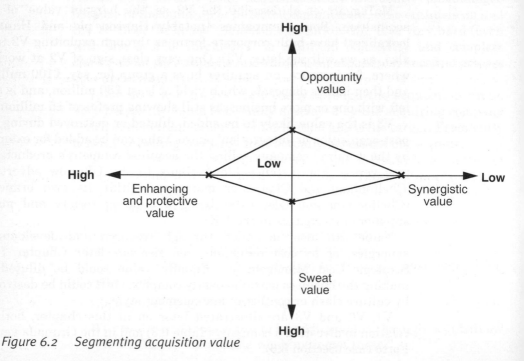

Figure 6.2   Segmenting acquisition value

assumed synergies prove feasible? Was the opportunity stream (and value) as attractive and as reachable as was originally thought? Did we make the cost base and assets 'sweat' as hard (and as quickly) as we anticipated?

This second way of segmenting value maps easily onto our V1, V2, V3 framework as follows (see Table 6.1):

Finally, managers should also explore a level of analysis below by examining the value and cost drivers at work in the acquired company. This is needed in order to understand the internal and external factors (for more on value and cost drivers refer to Chapter 7 – Strategic Cost Management).

6.3   *The search process – and acquisition criteria*

A frequent question from managers eager to acquire a new business is:

'Where do I find a company to acquire?'

An obvious place to start is an acquisition broker's or merchant bank – institutions who maintain a list of companies which someone is trying to sell.

The disadvantage of this approach is that it is an emergent strategy which, in the wrong hands, can end up with no real 'strategic fit' at all.

Another perspective is that:

'Unless you know the market (and probably the company) already, then you are unlikely to have sufficient competitive advantage to add value to the target.'

Unless you are looking for an acquisition where the value is essentially 'sweat value', or one where there are under-valued assets, a broadly ranging search is unlikely to yield real value.

Table 6.1   *Acquisitions and value segmentation*

	V1	V2	V3
Enhancing and protective value	N/A	N/A	Value of integration
Opportunity value	Net value of existing opportunity stream	N/A	Net present value of emerging opportunity stream
Synergistic value	N/A	N/A	Value of integration
Sweat value	N/A	Assumed business sales	Value of cost savings realised and asset sales

(N/A = not applicable)

Usually a Porter's five forces analysis of your various market places will yield some potential acquisition targets. This could be in the form of suppliers, channels to market, entrants or rivals. Competitor analysis can obviously identify more specific opportunities. Also, by examining your business value system you should be able to identify gaps in your value-adding activities you may be able to acquire, or strengths which you can apply to a weaker company.

In short, it is wise to use strategic analysis to tease out a small number of acquisition candidates rather than to go on a widely ranging acquisition hunt.

When you have finally come up with a small list of candidates, *then* is the time to apply your acquisition criteria to sort out which one may be worth approaching. These criteria are best expressed as acquisition 'do's and don'ts', rather than as bland criteria.

An example of criteria for acquisition in the Financial Services industry is as follows:

Acquisition 'do's'

- we must be able to negotiate a change of name (to the group)
- it must be of sufficient size (current profitability of over £5 million per annum) to be worth doing
- it must be a leader (as benchmarked by customers) in its particular niche
- we must be able to keep its management, who must be strong.

Acquisition 'don'ts'

- it must not be dominated by a key individual
- the culture must not be rather different from our own
- we will not pay over £50 million for the acquisition.

6.4   *The deal*

6.4.1   *Pricing the deal*

First of all, we need to consider the pricing of the deal. Pricing of an acquisition is again an art rather than a science. Managers typically yearn for a simple and mechanistic way of valuing and pricing an acquisition but this proves elusive for a variety of reasons.

First, managers must separate in their minds what an acquisition might be worth to them, what they might offer tactically for the deal, and also what a 'walk-away from' price might be.

Second, valuing an opportunity needs to be tackled from several angles. To begin with, an assessment of asset value may provide one perspective on the value of an acquisition. The book value of net assets may be very approximate, however, and some have recommended instead the use of written-down value of replacement assets. But in many cases the asset value may be considerably divergent from the fundamental economic value of the business. This is because of the acquired company's ability (present and future) to generate cash.

Therefore it is imperative to look also at the cash-generating capability of the business. Discounted cash flow (DCF) techniques offer managers a more theoretically robust way of evaluating these cash flows (4). But managers again need to beware how they arrive at assumptions which these projects are based on, for example, how any assumed 'terminal value' for the end of the time horizon of detailed forecast is derived. This can frequently form the majority of a deal's net present value. (More generally, you need to revisit the lessons of Chapter 5 on strategic investment decisions, especially in identifying the key uncertainties and then – and only then – doing sensitivity analysis.)

Further, a popular (and perhaps the most popular) method of evaluation is the use of market-based methods. For example, a company earning £10m (post tax) might be in a sector which characteristically has a price divided by earnings of eight (this is called the p/e ratio). On a p/e basis a valuation of the company might thus be worth £10m x 8 or £80m. But the p/e method is crude from a number of points of view, including:

- the base year may not be representative of longer-term trends

- historical accounting performance is backward, rather than future looking

- financially measured profits may be misleading. Lesser instances than Polly Peck, the Maxwell Group in the UK, and others are more widespread than perhaps is believed – and these were after all *public* companies – private companies may be even more suspect generally

- the current level of p/e's may be subject to hype in the acquisition market-place.

Returning now to the distinction between negotiating price, walk-away price and ultimate value to the business we see that:

- all methods of appraisal can be used in negotiating to present a value for a business in accordance with your own negotiating interests (for example, if using DCF, use a deliberately high discount rate – few managers *really* understand the basis of how the cost of capital is arrived at)

- a walk-away price does not have to equate with the ultimate value to the acquirer. For example, if you can afford to pay £200 million and are able still (just) to beat your cost of capital, this still means you have a *zero* net present value. To add value through acquisition you need to generate a *positive* and not a break-even net present value. When the acquisition chase reaches its crescendo, it is tempting to 'go all out' to 'win' the acquisition

- price may well be determined by competitive conditions – what is the 'target' likely to be worth to other potential acquirers? And what is their strategic intent and likely underlying psychology?

Ultimately, an acquisition is therefore worth:

'whatever someone is prepared to pay for it'.

6.4.2 *The negotiation process*

Even where an acquisition target does have a strategic logic, it is easy to dilute and destroy a considerable part of the added value of an acquisition simply through the negotiation process. Taking the ten most important imperatives of the deal process their likely impact on financial value, together with the pitfalls, are shown in Figure 6.4.

One particular point (number four) worth amplifying is about looking out for concealed (or half-concealed) 'skeletons'. Typical examples of 'skeletons' of value destruction include:

- products whose life-cycle could be ended prematurely
- disputes over ownership of technology
- insecure access to technology
- pending disputes with former employees
- large contracts which have run into trouble
- contingent costs associated with physical property
- overseas operations over which there is rather loose control, or which are ineffectually established
- new products about to be launched which do not really fit market requirements
  and so on…

The process of 'due diligence' (which involves going systematically through a large number of preconceived questions) aims to surface those black holes. But because the process of due diligence is still typically based on a generic list of questions (with some tailoring) it is still easy to miss new manifestations of 'deal skeletons'. Due diligence needs to be supplemented by the 'nose' of the acquirer, and particularly by the acquiring team's tenacity.

Further, traditional due diligence focuses especially on the more operational, contractual and legal aspects of the target. Where marketing and technological areas are covered, this is frequently addressed from a more internal, rather than an external, perspective. The downside to this is that *strategic* aspects of due diligence may be easily overlooked. Yet strategic vulnerability (for instance new competitor entry, new product failures) can have a profound impact on value.

Returning now to our fifth point, unless you keep an ongoing track of deal value you can lose sight of whether deal potential has fallen below your 'walk away' level. Sixth, the negotiation process can become dry and tedious and you may need to exercise patience with detail. Certain areas of detail (like tax) can have a significant impact over both the effective cost of the deal and over post-acquisition *new cash inflows*.

Table 6.2   *Managing the deal process*

Deal process imperatives	Pitfalls – if imperatives are not managed
1. Be clear about what, and what is not negotiable	Your benefits (and value) are continually eroded
2. Manage areas which are negotiable to your tactical advantage	You fail to capture (and lose) tactical deal advantages
3. Do not allow ambiguity to persist until too late	Essentials are not met or are diluted
4. Identify 'skeletons' remorselessly – that is things wrong with the business – or things which might go wrong	Value destruction is likely to occur
5. Keep ongoing track of deal value (and cost)	You don't get the value which you thought you would
6. Don't become impatient with apparent minutiae	You may pay more tax, incur more risk and ultimately bear unexpected liabilities
7. Limit your room to manoeuvre during integration (or give shaky promises to managers)	Integration becomes a bumpy ride and destroys or dilutes value
8. Do not give in to time pressure	You give away value which you could have had
9. Do not display over-enthusiasm	Your negotiating strength is undermined and you fail to extract tactical benefits
10. Avoid becoming over-committed	You overlook key downsides, pay too much and are unprepared for integration difficulties

Seventh, it may be tempting to give promises on the manner of integration (especially in management positions) when this might tie your hands unduly. Where you subsequently do a 'U-turn' on what you have agreed – or even tentatively suggested – this can generate an unpleasant and damaging fall-out.

Finally, there are many issues which need to be addressed in managing the *dynamics* of the deal process. The combination of time pressure, over-enthusiasm, and poorly managed commitment to the deal can prove to be a fatal strategic and financial cocktail (these are points eight, nine and ten in Table 6.2). Unless the 'momentum' of the deal is managed rigorously, then the potential value of the deal can turn sour.

Having looked at acquisitions from an *acquirer* perspective, let us now look at them from a *divestor* perspective.

6.4.3   Lessons for the divesting company

Most acquisitions guides contain a lot of advice on how to *acquire* but relatively little on how to *divest*. This is perhaps a reflection of the enthusiasm managers often have for acquisitions (seen as being a 'good thing') whilst divestment is seen as being embarrassing (a 'bad thing').

Clearly, divesting companies need to turn around all we have said about managing acquisitions. Ten lessons for shareholders and managers considering divestment (to the vendor) are shown in Figure 6.5 (distinguishing V1, V2 and V3 elements).

6.5   Acquisition integration and learning

6.5.1   Integration and value creation and destruction

The integration phase (5) is one where value is actually diluted or destroyed rather than created. This may be due to a variety of reasons, for instance:

- integration plans may be left to emerge and, if deliberate, are inadequately thought through to deal with obstacles to change

- there may be an abrupt change in management style, leading to lower morale and business performance rather than improved performance

- alternatively, there may be no real change in the management when one is badly needed, leading to drift

- the acquisition period itself is a distracting time for incumbent management. There may be a period of months or longer when new developments are deferred and costs are unwisely cut. During this period the normal attention to customer delivery may be lost

Table 6.3   *Ten lessons for the divesting owners/management*

1. What features of the market environment can you emphasise as being attractive (especially the growth drivers)? (V1)

2. What past competitive strengths can you identify and extrapolate out into the future, emphasising dominance or near dominance in key segments? (V1)

3. What is your future opportunity stream and what would it be worth as an upside if you had more funds to invest (ie from the acquirer)? (V1)

4. How can you create real or imagined rivalry for a deal and which new parent would it be worth most to? (V2)

5. What is the *lowest* cost of capital which could be used to discount our cash flows (and how could we justify this)? (V2)

6. What is the *highest* realistic terminal value – at the end of the forecast time horizons, and how can we justify this? (V2)

7. How can we best convey the impression that we are not in a hurry to do a deal – and we might not need to do one anyway? (V2)

8. What are the particular agendas on the acquisition team's minds (especially personal and political), and how can we exploit 'loose bricks' in the acquisition team's bid strategy? (V2)

9. What synergies with the acquirer's business value system (real or imagined) can you envisage and what 'best value' can be put on these? (V3)

10. What is the 'best case' for achieving 'sweat value' for integration and how can this be built into *our plans and forecasts* – 'we will do it anyway'? (V3)

- new management might impose its own 'way of doing things' (or 'paradigm' – see *Exploring Corporate Strategy*, Section 7.3.2, page 310) and thus damage the acquisition's competitive strength

- key staff may leave, feeling (rightly or wrongly) that their career prospects are blunted.

The integration phase is most important too, as it is during this period when the acquirer has most opportunity to learn from the acquisition. This learning should obviously deal with the post-acquisition performance of the acquisition – financially and strategically. But it should also cover the acquisition process itself. 'How difficult and speedily did we integrate the acquisition relative to our expectations?' is a central question.

Integration will be taken up as an issue once again when we meet the Granada versus Forte case in Section 6.6.

6.5.2   *Surfacing acquisition investment – the iceberg model*

Before we leave acquisition theory, we need to take a broader look at scoping the acquisition investment. This needs to be explored during the strategy and objectives-setting phase, and during screening, the deal-making stage, and during integration.

Besides strategy and deal-making, we should also recognise the importance of scoping the full investment requirement required by the strategy. It is useful to imagine this investment as a kind of 'iceberg' with some parts visible, but where a quite substantial chunk of investment is dimly visible or virtually invisible.

Managers frequently underestimate the investment required to:

- actually enhance the company's competitive position
- exploit both the existing and emergency opportunity stream
- harness synergies and reduce costs.

The tendency of managers to underestimate acquisition investment can be represented in the 'iceberg' model of investment (see Figure 6.3). Using the 'iceberg model', newcomers to the acquisition process see the deal cost (and some post-acquisition investment) reasonably clearly. These 'early learners' may not, however, appreciate the full extent of those costs, nor of the extent of integration costs and destruction costs which might also exist.

Figure 6.3 displays our iceberg of acquisition investment. Although the purchase price and transaction costs are mostly visible, deeper still a whole raft of costs including integration costs and the scale of future investment may be partially recognised. All too often any financial model used to appraise an acquisition (and the underlying mind-set of the acquirer) is based on the kind of thinking shown in Illustration 6.1.

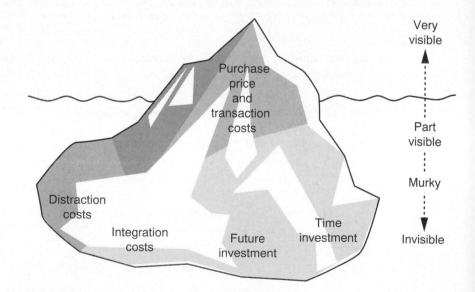

Figure 6.3   *The iceberg of acquisition investment*

Strategy in action

illustration 6.1

Valuing an acquisition

Acquisitions are often valued on the basis of cash flows of the existing business (and future improvements which the acquirer plans to make) but without factoring-in incremental investment needed.

The value of the acquisition is estimated conventionally as:

	£ million
Discounted cash flow from current operations and future strategy (from post integration)	= 135
Less total deal costs	= (97)
Net present value	38

But it should be estimated as:

	£ million
Discounted cash flow from current operations and future strategy (post integration)	= 135
Less total deal costs	= (97)
Less present value of all *future* investment requirements both to *deliver* strategic development and *protect* existing position	= (25)
Net present value	13

The 'investment costs' in Illustration 6.1 should also include some hard to assess, but nevertheless important, costs, including distraction costs and the costs of time investment. This is explored in a short illustration (6.2 overleaf) on BMW and Rover.

Having now set the scene for managing acquisitions both strategically and for shareholder value, we are now well placed to examine the complex case of Granada versus Forte.

Case study 6.1

Granada and Forte – the anatomy of an acquisition

6.1.1 Introduction

Strategic Financial Management is something which is of profound importance to managers and shareholders. The Granada–Forte battle shows decisively that strategy and shareholder value are closely

Strategy in action

illustration 6.2

BMW'S acquisition of Rover

In 1994, BMW acquired Rover – to the almost unanimous acclaim of the financial press. However, given the huge investment requirement of Rover – to complete the repositioning begun in the late 1990s, it would seem that BMW's shareholder value was significantly diluted, with very little return this side of the year 2000.

When BMW acquired Rover Group at a cost of £800 million in 1994, press commentators, in the main, felt this to be a 'good deal'. Since that time BMW's investment plans appear to have increased considerably, to the extent that investment by Rover has now doubled compared to its period of ownership by British Aerospace. So what is a 'cheap deal'? If we look at the higher level numbers for the Rover acquisition we have:

	£m
Initial deal cost	800
Investment over 5 years to revamp the product range 5 x £500 million	2,500
	3,300

Although BMW has been famous for taking a longer-term view, Rover's profits (admittedly on a conservative, German accounting basis) are expected to be low for a number of years to come. More recent press comments (*Car Magazine* (6)) have pinpointed the likelihood that BMW has significantly underestimated the investment required (and the time) to give Rover a genuinely strong, competitive position.

Indeed, the *Financial Times* (25 March 1997) disclosed that a reduction in the *loss* at Rover had enabled BMW Group to make a 16 per cent improvement in its profits. But if Rover were stripped out of these results, BMW's profits would have been doubled. Also, BMW's share price (as of March 1997) was at the same level as it was when it had acquired Rover in 1994. (In this period of nearly three years one would have hoped for a significant increase, especially for a strategically healthy business like BMW.) This performance underlines the dilutive effect Rover has had – both financially and strategically – on BMW.

intertwined. It also highlights that management face penalties for managing both strategy and value effectively, whether this is Forte (before its acquisition) or Granada (after its acquisition) (7).

Forte, a leisure conglomerate, fell prey in 1996 to Granada plc. Granada made a convincing case to Forte's shareholders that they could add more value to the Forte portfolio through disposal of some businesses, and through post-acquisition integration. This case highlights the need to manage a corporate portfolio for value – or another group might take over the job from you.

In 1995 Forte's turnover stood at £1,789 million (with net profits before tax of £127 million). In 1995 Granada had overtaken Forte with an impressive operating profit of £388 million, with operations principally in the UK.

Forte, by contrast, had extensive international operations. It had hotels in North America, the Caribbean, South America, Africa, the Middle and Far East, Australasia, Europe and Moscow.

Forte's major hotel brands included:

- exclusive hotels (18 hotels, 3,600 rooms)
- Forte Meridian (85 hotels, 23,400 rooms)
- Forte Posthouse (80 hotels, 10,000 rooms)
- Forte Heritage (52 hotels, 2,600 rooms)
- other hotels (12 hotels, 6,200 rooms)
(Source: Forte Defence Document, 1995)

Our full case study is now set out as follows:

- Forte's current strategic and financial position
- Granada's turnaround and strategic intent
- attacking the ramparts – the Granada bid
- repelling the invaders – Forte's defence
- overcoming the resistance – Granada's final push
- what business was Forte really in?
- counting the spoils – some lessons.

6.1.2 *Forte's current strategic and financial position*

Forte's 1995 Annual Report and Accounts began with a confident statement from its Chairman Sir Rocco Forte:

'We have embarked on a strategy of building powerful hotel and restaurant brands through effective marketing, focused geographical expansion, innovative product development on a high customer service orientation amongst our people.'

Reading this statement one might be forgiven for wondering *how* Forte became so vulnerable. Profit before tax was in the year ending 1995 £127 million, 65 per cent up on the previous year. Earnings per share were up 80 per cent. But Forte Group's past track record was not so impressive. Table 6.4 shows highlights from the past five years.

Case study 6.1

Table 6.4   Forte plc – summary results 1991–1995

	1995 £m	1994 £m	1993 £m	1992 £m	1991 £m
Sales:					
Continuing operations	1789	1638	1475	1440	1524
Discontinued operations	—	468	1246	1222	1117
	1789	2106	2721	2662	2641
Operating profit:					
Continuing operations	258	203	173	154	240
Discontinued operations	—	22	54	50	49
Net profit	258	225	227	204	289
Net interest	(131)	(148)	(167)	(143)	(111)
	127	77	60	61	178
Profits on disposals less losses	—	34	93	(17)	(2)
Profit after interest, before tax (1)	127	111	153	44	176
Total net assets (2)	2464	2352	2718	3020	3052

Return on net assets
(1) divided by (2) 5.1% 4.7% 5.6% 1.4% 5.7% (weighted average = 4.5%)

Clearly, Forte had gone through a period of strategic drift followed by a deliberate strategy which was only partly realised. But although a recovery in earnings was underway (by shedding its less profitable turnover) the question was: was this recovery being pushed as quickly and as effectively as was possible? Could the value of Forte's portfolio be released either by more effective management or by selling the business on to another parent? But clearly the historical performance (to 1995) might not reflect the underlying value of the business – both in terms of potential cash streams and asset value. This again reinforces the point that the base year for constructing future financial projections is critical in valuing the business.

Forte's Hotels operated in 60 countries with 940 hotels (with 97,000 rooms) and 600 restaurants. They included more exclusive hotels like Meridian and the Savoy, and the more lower/middle market Forte Posthouse and 115 budget Travelodges.

The restaurant businesses included the Little Chef and Happy Eater chains, which dominate the British roadside, and the motorway Welcome Breaks.

Forte thus presents itself as a relatively diverse group with a variety of generic strategies within its portfolio, including:

- differentiated – focus (Savoy/Meridian) to
- cost leadership – broad (Little Chefs)
- cost leadership – focus (Travelodge)

The operating profit of Forte's businesses breaks down as follows:

Forte – Operating profits

	1995 £m	1994 £m
Hotels	176	136
Restaurants	82	67
	258	203

The hotel businesses' turnover and operating profits break down as follows:

Forte – Sales – Hotels only

	1995 £m	1994 £m
London	232	204
Other UK	421	401
Total UK	653	605
International	359	337
	1012	942

Forte – Operating profit – Hotels

	1995 £m	1994 £m
London	69	53
Other UK	81	70
Total UK	150	123
International	26	13
	176	136

These profit improvements were due to improvements in volumes (occupancy up by six per cent) but average rates only increased by two per cent indicating price rises just under the level of inflation.

Case study 6.1

Meanwhile the restaurant businesses' results were:

Forte – Sales – Restaurants

	1995 £m	1994 £m
UK	584	558
Europe	70	64
	654	622

Forte – Operating profit – Restaurants

	1995 £m	1994 £m
UK	74	60
Europe	8	7
	82	67

These improvements were partly due to improved margins of 12.5 per cent (from 11 per cent) and higher average spend in roadside restaurants.

In summary, prior to Granada's bid, Forte had achieved a good deal to effect a short-term turnaround. Whether it had done enough is another question, because its financial performance was still less than satisfactory from a shareholder value point of view.

6.1.3 *Granada's turnaround and strategic intent*

In earlier times, Granada was run by the Bernstein family in what has been described as a 'paternalistic' way. When Robinson joined, Granada profits had fallen to £56.9 million. On the Wednesday of Granada's initial bid, profits stood at £351 million on turnover of £2.38 billion. This turnaround had made him extremely popular in the City. According to one institutional source, some watchers in the City believe that 'he (Gerald Robinson) walks on water'.

Granada had acquired Sutcliffe Catering and London Weekend Television and had produced major profit improvements there. This resulted in a wide spread of activities, as follows:

- broadcasting and production (LWT and Granada)
- other leisure (Granada, night clubs, studio tours)
- computer services
- TV rental
- motorway services (Granada, Pavilion, Burger Express)
- hotels (and lodges)
- theme parks

- workplace services
- contract catering (Sutcliffe)
- travel
- investments (BSkyB, ITN).

This proliferation led Forte to attack Granada as 'an acquisition-driven conglomerate'. But this may well mean that Granada excels in identifying and harvesting opportunities for achieving 'sweat value' by improving margins, reducing costs and disposing of undervalued assets.

6.1.4   *Attacking the ramparts – the Granada bid*

According to the *Sunday Times* (26 November 1995), Sir Rocco Forte, Chairman of Forte, could not believe the rumours that shortly Forte was to be in play as a bid target. Disbelieving these stories he chose not to alter his plans for a pheasant shoot in Yorkshire. Apparently he was still shaving at 8am when he heard that Granada had mounted a hostile £3.3 billion bid for the Group.

Ironically, just three months' previously Sir Rocco had played golf with Gerry Robinson, Granada's Chief Executive, who had (perhaps unsurprisingly) not even as much as hinted an interest in the Group. This particular bid was especially surprising to Forte because it seemed to them implausible that Granada had the skills to run a complex, international group like Forte. But was Robinson actually interested in running the whole group? Probably not, is perhaps the answer.

The £3.3 billion bid valued Forte shares at 328p a share, thus valuing Forte at 25 times current earnings. This represented a 19 per cent premium to Forte's pre-bid share price. Immediately, Forte's shares soared 71p to 346p, 19p over Granada's initial offer price. First impressions in financial markets were therefore that 'Forte's independence is doomed' and that Granada would bid more.

Forte's own projections of Granada's post-acquisition gearing estimated this as being over 200 per cent (up from 50 per cent prior to the acquisition), and that debt would soar to over £3.1 billion (Source: Forte bid defence document, 1995). This raised the question of 'would Granada become a highly geared, forced seller of assets at distressed prices?' Granada felt this level of gearing would be both temporary and manageable. Forte's view was that Granada would find it extremely tough to recoup value.

Granada's initial acquisition strategy was to:

- achieve a quantum improvement in Forte's marketing and cost controls (especially of overheads and through purchasing economies)
- dispose of Forte's 68 per cent stake in the Savoy Hotel Group

- dispose of Forte's motorway service stations, Lillywhites (sporting groups) and other minor businesses
- rejuvenate the restaurant businesses with better pricing and positioning (especially at the Little Chef and Happy Eater chains)
- increase prices at Posthouse and Travelodge chains by 20–25 per cent
- achieve significant purchasing economies.

Forte's posture was therefore that the bid was entirely opportunistic and that Granada brought nothing of value to the Group. (Granada might well have claimed that the bid was just very well timed.) Forte also felt that if disposals were appropriate then these could be managed by Forte itself. Forte also accused Granada of having no experience of running an international hotels business.

A major institutional shareholder, Mercury Asset Management ('MAM') held a major stake in both companies of:

- 12.5 per cent of Forte
- 14.8 per cent of Granada

So how MAM chose to play its cards was a key factor influencing the outcome of Granada's hostile bid. Further, Sir Rocco Forte who was *both* Chairman and Chief Executive of Forte may not have spent enough time communicating with his key institutional shareholders as perhaps he might .

Questions that investors like Mercury Asset Management needed to ask themselves to be persuaded to back the Granada bid were:

- was Robinson's Granada the best qualified management to rejuvenate Forte's brand names? The *Financial Times* (7 December 1995) asked, 'Was Granada management such a magic quality that it could work well in different industries?'

- did the Granada move hark back to the period of macho deal-making associated with the by now unfashionable period of the conglomerate?

- was Granada's progress on the earnings front at least partially due to a number of large restructuring provisions following past acquisitions? And was Robinson's record for improving the performance of acquired companies actually based on sound, longer-term strategic development?

- would the highly cash-generative television business of Granada face cash flow dilution from the more capital hungry, low cash yield and cyclical business of hotels?

- were Granada's finances sufficiently strong to support a bid on this scale?

- Granada's own net worth of a mere £585 million appeared small against Forte's net assets of £2.5 billion. Granada would need to borrow around £1.5 billion. If one combined the net assets of the businesses following the acquisition these would shrink from £3 billion to £1.6 billion (figures per the *Financial Times*, 7 December, 1995), whilst combined borrowings would rise from £1.9 billion to £3.3 billion. This produced a gearing of 173 per cent (which is £3.3 billion divided by £1.9 billion (times 100).

6.1.5 Repelling the invaders – Forte's defence

By late December 1995 Forte moved remarkably fast to repel Granada. Especially given the time scales in which it had responded, its bid defence was an impressive feat. Sir Rocco had put forward an apparently credible number of measures, including:

- a plan to sell its restaurant business and the Travelodge chain of budget hotels to Whitbread for over £1 billion
- a revaluation of its hotels to £3.1 billion (ten per cent above its estimated value in January 1994)
- an increase in its dividend (which was cut to 7.5p from 9.9p in January 1993. This dividend was last raised five years' previously).

The proposed disposal to Whitbread included 364 Little Chef and 68 Happy Eater roadside restaurants, 30 French and 30 British service stations, and 127 Travelodge hotels. This deal, in effect, increased the pressure on Granada to raise its bid. From Forte's point of view these disposals would have virtually wiped out Forte's £1.2 billion debt (including lease-backs), assuming no repayment of shareholders' capital.

In effect, Forte, by unbundling its own business portfolio, sought to outdo Granada in unlocking the value trapped inside the Group. But the real questions were: could Forte do a more effective job in generating synergistic value, sweat value and value created by improving and developing competitive position?

Additional parts of the bid defence package unfolded in early 1996. In the *Financial Times* (2 January 1996), it was disclosed that Forte also planned:

- to make a special dividend or share buy-back (of around 20 per cent) if the sale of various businesses went through to Whitbread
- to conduct a major expansion of its Meridian chain of hotels (these hotels were acquired from Air France in late 1994).

The *Financial Times* (3 January 1996) even suggested that the total package of defensive measures actually put 'Forte ahead on points'. Forte also complained that Granada was buying in just at the point of an upswing.

But Forte's defence document also disclosed some damaging facts:

Case study 6.1

its top hotels accounted for *one-third* of total assets but contributed just over 14 per cent of operating profits.

6.1.6   *Overcoming the resistance – Granada's final push*

On 9 January 1996, Granada increased its offer for Forte from £3.24 billion to £3.74 billion, presenting this revised bid as a 'knock-out blow' (*Financial Times*, January 1996). Granada also announced the early sale of Forte's Meridian hotels (assuming their bid was successful). Granada's bid of £3.74 billion was still some margin below Robinson's *walk-away from price* at which Granada would have been indifferent as to whether the bid went ahead or not.

Granada's cost savings in the first year were also estimated at £100 million. The cost savings included the (inevitable) closure of Forte's London headquarters and the sale of the Forte corporate jet. Ironically, Granada took Forte's own figures of £24 million of cost savings and then simply added 'how we can better this'. Also, several months after the actual deal press comment appeared to the effect that 'there is no sign of Granada selling the corporate jet'. Besides these areas of performance improvement, Granada also assumed a saving of five per cent of purchasing costs. In effect, Granada applied – at least to some extent – strategic cost management in reducing the cost base of Forte businesses.

6.1.7   *What business was Forte really in?*

Interestingly, Granada and Forte thus came up with very different answers to the questions of:

What businesses should Forte be in? and
How should these maximise shareholder value?

Forte	**Granada**
'An international hotel group with spread between differentiation and best cost strategies'	'A selected portfolio of mainly UK restaurant businesses and lower/middle end hotels'

Granada thus seems to have opted for a mass market focus with selectively higher prices and lower costs. Forte has opted for a spread of operations across the spectrum of the hotel industry – and with an enormous span of market positionings.

The *Financial Times* (10 January 1996) questioned whether Forte's decision to retain the up-market hotels might have lumbered it with a fundamental, financial disadvantage given the low return on net assets from these hotels. Another liability retained by Forte was Sir Rocco Forte's continuance as both Chairman and Chief Executive –

twin roles being frowned on by the City.

We now focus on what Granada actually proposed to retain (and improve) (from the *Financial Times*, 10 January 1996):

- Forte Posthouse
- Forte Travelodge
- Little Chef
- Happy Eater
- Cote France

Granada intended to sell both Forte's Exclusive chain of hotels and the Meridian chain. Surprisingly, after the acquisition, Granada decided to keep the Meridian (*The Times*, 23 May, 1996). This apparently surprised City analysts, and also Sir Rocco Forte, who had been hoping to buy both the Exclusive and the Meridian chains.

Granada adopted a piecemeal disposal strategy for the Exclusive Hotels. Although it achieved a good price (£86 million) for the Hyde Park Hotel (£16 million over book value), by late 1996 it became apparent that other properties would be much harder to sell at good prices. (*The Times*, November 1996, described the Exclusive portfolio as a 'mixed one'.)

The final piece of the jigsaw puzzle was Granada's tax planning. Granada offered a cash alternative to declaring a special dividend. The attraction of this was that where shareholders were not tax-paying this offered a tax credit (or, in simple terms, *hard cash*) of 25 per cent of the special dividend received.

6.1.8   The personal battle

There was also a very personal dimension to the battle. As the *Sunday Times* (14 January 1996) highlighted, both Sir Rocco Forte and Gerald Robinson were battling for their personal reputations. Forte, obviously smarting from being taken off-guard by Granada, protested that 'all they were doing was to accelerate our plans by 12 months'. Gerry Robinson, for his part, was quoted as saying, acidly, 'we have seen more strategy from Forte in the past couple of weeks than we have seen in the last ten years' (the *Money Programme*, BBC, 1995).

6.1.9   Digesting the deal – acquisition integration

By late 1996 Granada had moved fast to integrate Forte's businesses. This included:

- cost cutting at Head Office
- price rises in the Travelodge chain, and testing out of Travelodge city centre sites
- new menus at both Little Chef and the Happy Eater (apparently

adding Burger King outlets has doubled average turnover – *The Times*, 7 October, 1996)
- the planned sale of the Exclusive Hotels for around £850 million
- a new management team was put into Meridian to manage the hotels as a group rather than individually
- extensions to Posthouse hotels, increased turnover.

Granada has certainly moved very fast to harvest the value potential of V3 (especially by generating sweat value), and in 1997 more disposals were made. Personal visits, however, to Granada outlets indicate patchier service than under Forte.

6.1.10   *Counting the spoils and the dead – some lessons*

Granada's final blow (the offer of over £3.7 billion) proved decisive. Forte succumbed to the revised Granada bid but this left Granada with an extremely difficult challenge: delivering shareholder value in the aftermath of a damaging corporate battle. The *Financial Times* (24 January 1996) highlighted the immediate crisis faced by Granada: how to salvage morale within the Forte Group. Granada's three major challenges (on top of the morale issue) were:

- integrating the parts of the business Granada wants to keep
- selling off Forte's up-market hotels
- reducing Granada's debt, standing at the consummation of the bid at an uncomfortable £3.5 billion.

Following the agreed bid, Gerald Robinson announced his plans to introduce Burger King outlets into at least 100 Little Chefs (to increase their youth appeal). This, apparently, proved to be a very successful move – with large increases in turnover being achieved.

With a rapid rate of disposal and assuming a healthy free cash flow from combined business, debt was projected as falling to a more comfortable level by September 1997. This was projected to reduce gearing to just 70 per cent based on existing asset valuations.

So, Granada hopes to prove to its shareholders that it not only has avoided overpaying for Forte, but it also hopes to demonstrate that (without artificial, financial engineering) it can genuinely deliver shareholder value through its investment in Forte.

6.6   *Key lessons from Granada and Forte*

A number of key lessons can be drawn out of this case study. These include:

- strategy development, which is not very well focused and which is tenuously linked to shareholder value, ultimately gets 'found out'.

Case study 6.1

Forte's expansion in the late 1980s and before into becoming a complex leisure conglomerate exposed it to the severe competitive and financial pressures of the recession. Forte strove hard to recover from these external shocks. However, its management may not have challenged as hard as perhaps it might its ultimate business fundamentals

- a similar question mark hangs over Granada's motives in acquiring Forte. Granada's bid timing was only just 'timed right' as Forte was on a recovery path, and Granada had to pay in excess of 25 times the recently improved earnings for its businesses. A detached observer might well conclude that Granada's new business portfolio is *almost* as complex as the original Forte one. Unless there are further disposal plans we may have seen one corporate conglomerate merely replaced by another

- Forte's bid defence reflects a degree of astuteness which appears to have set Granada back. Forte made considerable capital out of the strategic attractiveness of its business, which any potential divestor should do – in order to get a really good price (or in this case to claim existing management can do a better job). Did Granada really think through Forte's counter moves (and how they would themselves respond to these counter moves)? This highlights the need to work out in some depth the deal negotiation strategy and tactics

- further, Granada's integration strategies for the rump of Forte's businesses are certainly radical, but are they sufficiently well thought through? In the press comment, the main focus is on the corporate wrestling match rather than on how the 'winner' will be able to cash in on his assumed trophy. Granada has a lean corporate team and it may find it difficult to achieve the assumed improvements as fully and as quickly as it expects.

We can now summarise the acquisition logic by going back to our acquisition value – V1, V2 and V3.

Table 6.5   Forte's acquisition value

Sources of V1	Sources of V2	Sources of V3
Hotels business – markets were growing, margins improving again.	Sell-off up-market hotels.	Marketing improvement and innovation.
Roadside restaurants had strong positions in relatively attractive markets.	Ready buyers for some of roadside restaurants.	Cost cutting and synergy management.
Improvements by Forte management now coming through.	Granada's deal-making skills.	Granada's integration skills.

6.7 Conclusion

Acquisitions are indeed a dangerous terrain both financially and strategically – especially for the 'early learner' type of manager. On the surface, acquisitions are primarily an issue of deal-making and financial engineering. Whilst these activities are clearly central of themselves they may not provide the complete recipe for adding shareholder value. In addition, managers need to do sufficient strategic thinking to anticipate *where* to add value post-acquisition, and also *how* they will achieve this during integration.

Although we have looked at acquisitions from a slightly different value-creation perspective than in earlier chapters, the fundamentals are the same. In particular analysis tools which are relevant here (as in earlier chapters) include:

- strategic management accounting (for mapping 'what businesses we are in') and life-cycle analysis). The Forte business portfolio did seem to be particularly diverse, but so too was Granada's

- Porter's five competitive forces and growth drivers (for evaluating the inherent attractiveness of specific markets or segments)

- the General Electric Grid (for positioning the business portfolio). Here we might well have seen Forte's Travelodges and Little Chefs having a strong competitive position, and being of medium market attractiveness. Some of the more exclusive hotels could be regarded as being average-weak competitive position and potentially low market attractiveness (because of low growth, cyclicality, and high competitive rivalry)

- analysing competitive advantage (and competitor analysis) –this helps to identify which businesses it is more worthwhile keeping

- the business value system (for identifying areas for breakthroughs in financial performance and synergies). For instance, what additional purchasing economies were available throughout the business portfolio?

- value and cost drivers – these help to identify the longer-term profit potential of the businesses and any areas where V3 can be generated during integration

- analysing interdependencies and the strategic project set. For example, this helps to identify all aspects of integration; during the integration Granada did not merely put up prices for its Travel Inn chain – it also invested in programmes to help managers to innovate more

- the uncertainty-importance grid (for surfacing external and internal assumptions, including integration)

- strategic financial accounting (for understanding the target's annual report and accounts, for instance Forte Group).

Acquisitions are therefore a major theatre of Strategic Financial Management. Not only do managers need to maintain strategic clarity and financial objectivity, they also need to keep their personal agendas and career ambitions in rein.

This necessitates a tighter integration between strategic *and* financial due diligence. It also requires setting post-acquisition measures which focus on the creation of longer-term shareholder value, rather than merely on very short-term profit enhancement. This in turn calls for appropriate rewards and recognition systems.

In the conduct of post acquisition management, the management of cost plays a major role. We now address how costs can be managed for both financial and competitive advantage in Chapter 7. Post acquisition integration and development also requires implementing strategic change.

6.8   Key questions

Key questions which you are now invited to address include:

1. Do acquisitions hold an unduly favoured role in your organisation (over organic development) and, if so, what are the consequences?

2. Equally, do you tend to think about the acquisition options as a part of opposing organic investment decisions?

3. Is your company typically better at creating V1, V2 or V3 value?

4. How does your organisation *monitor* whether it has captured the assumed value from acquisitions?

5. What are the strengths and weaknesses of your *acquisitions process* – particularly in identifying targets, data collection, target evaluation, and negotiation?

References

(1)   See *Exploring Corporate Strategy*, Section 7.3.2
(2)   Jemison D. B. and Sitkin S. B., *Acquisitions: The Process can be a Problem*, pp 107-116, Harvard Business Review, Boston, March–April 1996
(3)   McTaggart J. M., Kontes P. W., Mankins M. C., *The Value Imperative*, The Free Press, Macmillan, 1994
(4)   See *Exploring Corporate Strategy*, Chapter 8, and our Chapter 5
(5)   See *Exploring Corporate Strategy*, Section 7.3.2, especially the top of page 310
(6)   *Car Magazine*, September 1996
(7)   See *Exploring Corporate Strategy*, Illustration 5.1

effectively within the value chain (resulting, in effect, in the 'value drain'). Illustration 7.1 describes how British Airways had begun to tackle this issue in the late 1990s.

This brief overview of British Airways is important as it is essential, when seeking to manage the cost base strategically, to understand the external and internal strategic context.

Following this overview we now address:

- how can we learn from and use different management theories on cost? (Sections 7.2 to 7.5)
- the strategic cost management process (Section 7.6)
- lessons and conclusions.

We will continue to flesh out the notion of strategic cost management with reference to British Airways in Illustration 7.1. In order to manage both financial and competitive advantage simultaneously, we need to do a number of things:

- balance longer-term against shorter-term priorities in our allocation of resources
- ensure that where we make any cost reductions this only adds to, rather than subtracts from, the overall competitive advantage of the business
- make trade-offs between costs against value added (ie the idea of value-for-money and positioning on the 'strategy clock' which compares perceived added value and price (2)
- prioritise expenditure against both strategic and financial criteria
- identify, understand and manage those 20 per cent of key cost drivers (which represent 80 per cent of the most important areas of the cost base) based on the Pareto principle (see again, Chapter 3 on Strategic Management Accounting).

In order to manage an area of cost by looking at its total business implications, it is necessary to explore a number of complementary perspectives on cost.

The following section now gives an overview of different management perspectives on cost, derived from:

- strategic management
- financial management
- operations management
- organisational change.

7.2   *Cost – a strategic management perspective*

The areas in this section are covered extensively in *Exploring Corporate Strategy*. Our purpose here is to tease out the main issues relevant to managing the cost base strategically, yet giving sufficient

Strategy in action

illustration 7.1
Strategic cost management at British Airways

British Airways has implicitly adopted the principles of Strategic Cost Management. BA has challenged the rationale of its entire resource base in a very radical way.

During the 1980s, British Airways (BA) staged a market turnaround by effecting major service improvements, by building on its brands and by developing its network. By the mid-1990s this strategy had yielded most of its potential value, although of course it was still amenable to continuous improvement. In September 1996 BA announced that it was considering a major reduction of staff in those activities which were not considered to be 'core' (or activities concerned with maintaining the more 'hygiene' aspects of customer value – see again Chapter 2). According to the *Independent*, 7 September 1996, BA planned to reduce its costs by £1 billion per annum. This entailed shedding up to 10,000 staff.

Activities seen as potential candidates for cost-saving under the banner of 'Step Change', included cargo handling and crew support. BA also aimed to cut costs by reducing the need for travel agents' commissions. They also seemed to be planning to run some of its peripheral routes via franchisees, thus avoiding the need for centralised management costs.

In the longer term, it was mooted that British Airways would simply fly aircraft and provide face-to-face contact with its customers. Interestingly this move occurred at a time when BA was generating record profits (£585 million in the last financial year) and had already achieved massive savings through purchasing deals, new working methods and by reduced labour costs. This highlights that costs can and should be harnessed effectively not just in tough or recessionary times but also in times which are more plentiful.

British Airways was very wise in thinking during 1996 about its *future* cost base, in case another recession might begin (over the next few years), or competitive intensity might increase substantially (or both). Indeed, according to the *Sunday Times* (27 September 1996), Robert Ayling, BA's Chief Executive saw trouble ahead from a combination of deregulation, lower fares and new competitors.

Clearly a big issue with this kind of initiative is the buy-in needed from the workforce. Although intuitively managers might feel it necessary to *impose* such a change, the rationale for change does need to be skilfully communicated. Also, it should still be feasible (if not essential) to get staff's fullest input into implementation plans.

background to those readers who are new to the *Exploring Corporate Strategy* series. Readers well acquainted with *Exploring Corporate Strategy* should thus focus primarily on the cost base implications of this section.

Cost is mentioned in a number of areas in the strategic management literature, for instance:

- the experience curve
- cost leadership strategies
- differentiation strategies
- competitor's costs – analysis
- the value chain and core competences.

7.2.1   *The experience curve*

Firstly, cost plays a role in the experience curve – which extrapolates the effect of learning experiences and physical economies of scale. The experience curve works as follows: as an organisation produces a particular product or service in greater and greater volumes, its unit costs tend to fall. In some industries, particularly where the end product or service is complex, and/or the process of production and delivery, this decline in costs can be dramatic.

In some industries the fall in costs can be so steep as to present a straight line over time against a log scale. But managers will more easily recognise the tendency for costs to actually fall in relative terms over time, and to do so first slowly then quickly (see Figure 7.1). This rate of decline of costs therefore occurs disproportionately over time in proportion to cumulative volume. The caveat here is that volume is not achieved at the expense of adding complexity – invariably dramatic cost reduction is achieved at least in part by simplification – of product, of process, or of both.

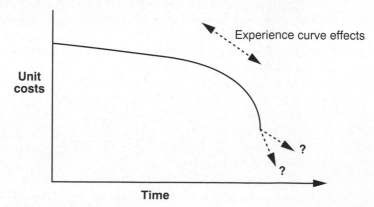

Figure 7.1   Unit cost reduction – over time

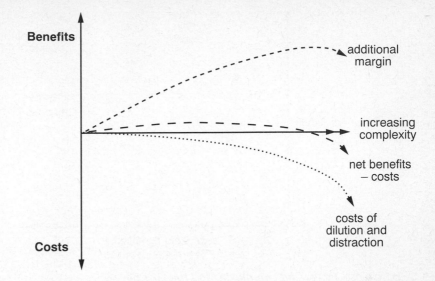

Figure 7.2   Anticipating the effects of business expansion – and increasing complexity

Experience curve effects can be of vital strategic and financial significance. If a company is able to achieve a relatively high market share early on in the development of a product or market then it can drive down its costs using the experience curve effect. This can be achieved by attaining a cumulative volume far in excess of its nearest competitor. Should an early lead therefore be established, then the benefits in terms of both competitive and financial advantage are also cumulative over time.

The impact of the experience curve needs to be evaluated on a case-by-case basis. Shank and Govindarajan (3) rightly point out that managers often make decisions to expand product line or volume which assume easy-to-reap economies of scale. Often the incremental profits (and cash flow) are elusive because this incremental business is not truly profitable (see Figure 7.2), where new products are introduced which generate some economies of scale. However, after a certain point of increasing complexity these benefits are negated by the escalating cost of distraction.

Profit improvements may also be elusive in this situation, but may nevertheless be measured because of inappropriate cost allocations through fixed or semi-fixed costs rising to sustain additional activity.

For instance, in Figure 7.3 the *measured* costs of an operation are perceived to fall as new products are introduced, because these resources are being supplied without charge from elsewhere in the organisation. Figure 7.3 also highlights the effect of 'lumpy' fixed costs. Although introducing one new product does not increase fixed costs,

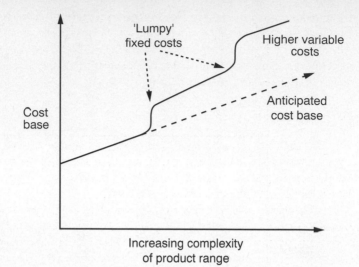

Figure 7.3   Increasing complexity and the cost base

increasing several new products does. So although the organisation appears to be increasingly profitable in the short run, this is an illusion in the long run.

Managing the experience curve effect is not something that you can easily address by sophisticated economic or financial modelling. It is best approached by creating a mini-scenario (sufficiently distant in the future) of the key cost drivers. This scenario should also contain some assumptions about the likely level of *complexity* of customer needs, products, services and processes. It is this very complexity which leads to the diversity which in itself dilutes the experience curve effect considerably.

So there are some major riders to the experience curve in pursuing SCM – managers should not delude themselves that higher volume and relative market share necessarily yield lower cost relative to competitors.

In British Airways' case, managers could fruitfully analyse their activities to determine where greater economies of scale could be achieved by out-sourcing rather than in-sourcing activities.

7.2.2   Cost leadership strategies

Following our discussion of the experience curve, this leads on naturally to the topic of cost leadership. According to Michael Porter (4), cost leadership is achieved only when a company has the lowest cost position in a particular industry (5). This does not necessarily mean that the cost leader has the lowest price (although low price and low cost are often closely associated in practice). This test of being the lowest cost player is a strenuous one. In practice where an industry is made up of a number of fragmented groups of players (for instance in retailing), it is often better to define cost leadership relative to a group of competitors (or 'strategic group').

7.2.3 Differentiation

A differentiation strategy also has major implications for cost management. Differentiation involves adding more real or perceived value to target customers relative to competitors – with costs slightly higher or on a par with key competitors.

BA has pursued a competitive strategy of differentiation since the mid-1980s, and would be unwise to undermine its service reputation and brand by reducing costs to the bone in key areas of customer value.

Where competitive rivalry has increased substantially (for instance in a maturing industry), companies are saddled with the challenge, however, of both improving service and value *and* reducing costs. Strategies to sustain advantage through differentiation need to be underpinned by strong cost management.

Frequently the process of ongoing reduction in the cost base is managed in part by publishing targeted reductions in the cost base for several years, rolling into the future, for example efficiency gains in the public services. Whilst possibly unsettling to many managers, this at least creates a climate for challenging cost. But rolling cost reductions do need external competitive justification rather than being arbitrary targets. Also they need to be made without undermining the competitive strategy. Cost programmes should thus be managed as an integral part of the strategic change process – to avoid damaging organisational capability.

With a differentiation strategy, the core value of the superior product or service should be delivered at a cost not substantially out of line with those competitors who occupy a similar strategic positioning (see position 4a) (6). This 'strategy clock' compares relative price with perceived added value. Additional costs over and above those of competitors are then tolerated and, indeed, are selectively encouraged if and only if they add disproportionate value to customers. This incremental value must then be harvested through premium price or additional volume, or through both.

A successful differentiator should therefore achieve a high value/cost leverage for those areas of cost which it has most discretion over (see, again, the Importance-Influence grid in Figure 3.7). Particularly important are aspects of service and product performance beyond the minimal requirements for becoming a viable competitor (ie above position 2 on the 'strategy clock'). For instance, in BA's case, management must thus test out these activities on a case-by-case basis, rather than forcing all activities to cut costs equally. This may mean deeper cuts in some areas and shallow ones elsewhere, or no cost cuts at all and even areas of more spending.

Where brand is an important means of achieving competitive advantage, a successful differentiator may also require a high relative market share to gain sufficient value/cost leverage for its advertising and promotional spend (A&P). Here we may see a virtuous cycle of extra cost in A&P leading to higher market share, economies of scale and lower operating cost.

With a differentiation strategy, the main emphasis will be on motivator factors *although hygiene factors (which are those factors that a customer expects to be in place at a minimal standard) must also be met*. For example, elaborating the Dyson case in Chapter 5, James Dyson was most liberal in his customer service arrangements. He was prepared to guarantee couriered delivery of a replacement machine in the unlikely event of a break-down, notwithstanding the cost. This is a clear example of a 'motivator' which would not have been expected by most customers and would also have added high perceived value. (In all probability, the actual cost of this guarantee was low, as Dyson had made sure – through his rigorous quality standards – that the machines rarely, if ever, broke down.)

7.2.4   Competitor's costs – analysis

Another key input from strategic management is that of competitor analysis. This can yield very powerful insights about relative cost levels. For example, at Dowty Case Communications (7) competitor analysis revealed that rivals were deploying much heavier sales teams on key accounts. Although at first sight this seemed to be more expensive, in fact sales costs relative to sales revenues at Dowty were higher because their hit rate was actually lower. The question for British Airways is thus:

> 'How are our competitors planning to reduce *their* cost base, and how will this position them against us in terms of customer value added?'

Figure 7.4 shows a classic situation where the company initially makes plans to reduce incrementally its cost base. Yet a key competitor *already has* a lower cost base – even though it services the same target customers. This company needs to think not only about meeting (and beating) the competitor's *current* cost base but also its *future* one.

This requires thinking through not merely the competitor's intent

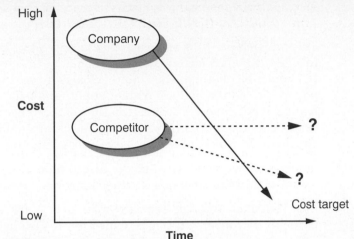

Figure 7.4   Competitive targeting of costs

(and its ability to implement that intent) but also how future competitive environment may change. This scenario will determine how much external pressure is put on the competitor to reduce its cost further. The Bank of Ireland calls this 'Managing costs competitively' or MC^2.

In order to assess a competitor's relative cost base, consider:

- what areas of cost are more important (in Pareto terms)?

- which areas of cost are more amenable to reduction or could be used to generate more value (either by yourself or your competitor, or both) – see again the Importance-Influence grid, Figure 3.7

- what are the key external and internal cost drivers in your competitor's business value system (for example, plant location, wage rates, product complexity)? For example, Dyson (in Chapter 5) could have easily established that Hoover's complex product range increased its costs in R&D, operations, sales and distribution, and administration

- what is your *best assessment* – given any publicly available data (from annual accounts or industry statistics) and proxies for hard information of the competitor's cost base? (For example, how many managers do they have across the functions? This helps to assess whether administrative overhead costs are higher or lower.) Also, what can data gleaned from third parties (for example, from suppliers to your competitors, or from their customers or distribution channels) tell you about their relative cost base?

Evaluating a competitor's cost base is thus very much a piece of detective work. But remember, you will never get an exact comparison of costs, and nor do you need it. Once the major strategic and financial insights have been gained, diminishing returns will set in.

7.2.5   *The value chain and core competences*

The value chain (8) is one way of exploring 'what business(es) we are in' and also what business(es) we should be in – from the inside out. It should be distinguished quite clearly from the more simplistic notion of 'added value'. Value chain analysis in strategic cost management involves looking at the company's value chain and its existing and potential fit with the value chains of both customers and suppliers. In practical terms this means examining:

- how a product or service makes direct reductions in cost (or extra value) within the customer's value chain; or

- how it makes indirect reductions in cost – for example by being particularly convenient to use, which in turn leads to time savings; or

- how the product or service enables the customer to extend his/her own value-adding activities. For example, a product or service may facilitate expansion of volume, or improvement in price or avoidance of discounts.

In this book we prefer to adopt the concept of the 'business value system' (see Chapter 2) over and above the value chain. This is because the 'business value system' is a more organic and naturally dynamic way of looking at value creation.

Porter's value chain is thus a first, albeit crude, step along the journey of identifying key business processes. Bundles of these processes can be viewed as mini-business units in their own right. BA has clearly put its value creating activities very closely under the microscope and said 'what cost base do we need to/could have?' rather than 'how do we manage from here?' It has done so by considering what its core competences are and should be in the future.

Besides core competences, there may be other competences from which a company can generate value. This may encourage it to *extend* its business value system to embrace more marginal activities (or its 'value domain' – see Chapter 2).

Often businesses build certain competences (like information systems, distribution or R&D) in order to service their own customer needs to a point where this becomes distinctive. This might suggest that the company might offer these distinctive competences as a marginal business to other companies in its own right. For instance, the computer company ICL built up a competence in strategic change facilitation internally. It then began to facilitate strategic change in other organisations, which led on to it charging consultancy fees for these services.

On the other hand, managers might see the case for re-examining this business function or process to see whether it is so crucial for longer-term competitive advantage and, if this is questionable, whether there is a case for sub-contracting out. (Here we are reducing, or shrinking, the business value system.)

Where the key value-creating activities are essentially 'hygiene' value drivers (see Chapter 2), there is a strong argument for considering contracting out. The decision on whether to contract in or out depends on a variety of factors, particularly:

- the direct and indirect benefits (both now and future)
- the direct and indirect costs (both now and future)
- the business risks (distinguishing the risks of managing the transition, which could be high, and the ongoing risks, which could be low).

It is crucial when considering this sensitive issue to examine the question:

'What are our options for doing the activity better, cheaper, simpler, and quicker in-house?'

In British Airways' case, will BA undermine its core competences by pursuing the 'step change initiative' as it is currently envisaged? This demands deep and objective understanding of BA's motivator and hygiene factors.

7.2.6 A summary

We have therefore seen that cost should and often does play a major role in shaping business strategies in practice. Costs are a very important ingredient of both internal, strategic analysis and also in considering external, competitive advantage. Cost analysis may also play a role in determining which industries, markets and market segments are inherently attractive to operate in, and how sustainable this attractiveness is likely to be. In British Airways' case 'step change' signals to shareholders much greater competitive pressure than that prevailing now. This has a fundamental and ongoing input into 'what business(es) we are in'.

7.3 A financial management perspective on costs

Traditional cost accounting focuses on setting budgets and standard costs, and upon subsequent monitoring and analysis of the variances. The purpose of this chapter is to distil from financial management the most appropriate techniques for managing costs strategically (rather than describing or critiquing traditional cost accounting).

7.3.1   Activity based costing

More useful from the point of view of strategic cost management is the critique on traditional cost accounting which occurred in the 1980s, principally by Kaplan (9). Kaplan argued that traditional management accounting systems produce misleading management information. Historically, costs were allocated in relation to the physical use of production assets – both capital and labour. But as the service element grew as a proportion of the value chain of most businesses, the traditional bases of cost allocation became increasingly irrelevant.

Kaplan's argument is that there are often more important activities which underpinned the value added within the production process than those associated with physical operations. To identify these activities, Kaplan proposed an alternative process which he named 'Activity Based Costing' or 'ABC'. The key steps of ABC (10) involve:

* firstly, managers need to understand how costs are generated (directly and indirectly) in the organisation – hence identifying the key cost drivers

* secondly, they then need to see whether processes can be simplified or changed in order to reduce costs or add more value (thus leading on into an embryonic form of business process re-engineering)

* thirdly, having re-designed business processes, they need to devise a method of tracking costs through monitoring the performance of a number of key performance indicators designed to measure the impact of key cost and value drivers.

Activity Based Costing approaches should not be seen as stand-alone but should be integrated with attempts to get a clearer view of what business(es) we should be in, and with business process re-engineering (11) (12). These management programmes are usefully placed under the banner of 'strategic cost management' to position them appropriately within the strategic development process. (In Illustration 7.3 we look at how an activity-based management programme can be targeted financially – as an example of evaluating cost programmes as a strategic investment decision.)

7.3.2   Micro analysis of cost drivers

The idea of cost drivers was introduced in our Chapter 2 on Managing for Value. We now take this useful notion a stage further.

The notion of 'cost drivers' is not self evident, either in theory or in practice. Porter (4) defines cost drivers as:

'A number of structural factors that influence cost.' (p 70)

He also lists a number of key cost drivers:

- economies of scale and learning effects
- patterns of capacity utilisation
- linkages and interrelationships
- integration
- timing
- discretionary policies
- location
- institutional factors.

These are relatively broad factors, and should not, as is argued by Kaplan (9), be mistaken for more operationally specific cost drivers. Kaplan recommends that we should concentrate on analysing the costs of primary activities between direct and indirect costs, then focusing on more specific cost driver categories particularly in terms of indirect costs. For example, depreciation and interest need to be traced to specific products (as suggested by Tomkins) (13).

In British Airways' case the structural factors are thus:

- in-sourced versus out-sourced activities and competences
- contractual relationships for out-sourcing
- distribution channels (especially the role of travel agents)
- information processes which co-ordinate the whole business value system effectively.

Probably it is fair to say that British Airways is closely following Marks and Spencer's model of being 'the manufacturer without manufacturing' (or an organisation with the competence to understand the manufacturing process as well as a real manufacturer, but which doesn't own manufacturing resources).

It is not always easy for managers to identify key cost drivers – principally because managers become too close to their business. In order to identify them it is frequently helpful to draw up a cost driver hierarchy.

A cost driver hierarchy which was done by Tesco (to evaluate cost drivers for its supermarket trolleys) is shown in Illustration 7.2 and Figure 7.5 (overleaf).

7.3.3 Cost programmes as strategic investment decisions

A second strand of thinking is that a large element of costs are actually, in effect, investment decisions (14). (See our earlier Chapter 5.) Yet so rarely do we see these longer-term cost programmes appraised as such – even by using relatively crude measures like payback. Strategic cost management thus draws from the techniques of Chapter 5, even though it is predominantly concerned with short- to medium-term resource allocation.

Strategy in action

illustration 7.2

Analysing the cost hierarchy

Cost drivers are those variables which directly or indirectly drive cash outlets

A technique for creating a hierarchy of cost drivers (see Figure 7.5) is to pose the following questions:

- what are the key stages in the cost life-cycle (in this case, initial investment versus operations)?

- what are the key things which push up costs (from a zero or low base)?

The corollary of the cost driver hierarchy is the value driver hierarchy. We could have done a similar hierarchy for the value drivers for a supermarket trolley. This would have addressed both value to the customer (and how this was harvested by Tesco), and value to Tesco (in enabling more sales to be achieved). The important thing to remember here is that in Strategic Cost Management one should never manage cost *in vacuo* from value.

Postscript: On 24 May 1997 (*The Times*), Tesco's new, hitherto secret, trolley was unveiled. This incorporated a device to ensure superior cornering and a guaranteed capability to go in a straight line. The trolley would not only be cheaper but have higher performance, and it is shown by *The Times* being independently tested by Jeremy Clarkson, the leading motor car commentator, who described it as 'the Tesco 225'.

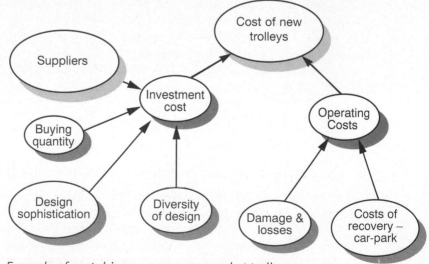

Figure 7.5   Example of cost drivers – new supermarket trolleys
By permission of Tesco

In reality there are many areas of cost where the bulk of the benefit is felt after the immediate, one-year budgetary period, especially in years two and three.

Examples of quasi-investment decisions include:

- acquisition costs of new customers (see also our later Illustration 7.5)
- advertising and promotion
- business process re-engineering
- culture change
- entry costs into new markets or segments
- major consulting projects
- management and organisational development
- product development
- research and development
- restructuring programmes
- systems development
- total quality management.

Managers can appraise their internal cost programmes as if they were investment decisions. For example, Illustration 7.3 shows how financial projections for a cost programme can be used as the basis of a business case. If managers use a business case approach to appraise cost programmes along these lines, then they might gain some interesting insights, for example:

- many cost programmes might provide a much faster payback and higher ratio of present value (of outlays) than many more tangible areas of investment
- some cost programmes have dubious benefits; many of which are largely claimed to be 'intangible'. When exposed to scrutiny, however, this intangible nature might be revealed to be due to their being poorly thought through and targeted. For example, in the scenario in Illustration 7.4 the activity-based management system might have been implemented but without thinking through the *specific* cost savings projects which might result
- on balance, a project with a shorter payback should be preferred to one with a similar NPV (especially if there are opportunities to do other similar projects) (see Figure 7.6 on page 188). Here value can be 'turned-over' faster than with slower payback projects. A proviso, however, is that managers should avoid unbalancing the portfolio of cost programmes/projects. This is especially relevant where valuable projects with harder-to-quantify but nevertheless genuine benefits are put at an unfair disadvantage.

In Illustration 7.3 we examine the prioritisation of cost programmes.

In Illustration 7.4 we look at the financial appraisal of a cost reduction programme.

Strategy in action

illustration 7.3
Evaluating different cost management programmes

Conventional theory suggests that projects should be ranked primarily on the basis of their net present values. However, there may be circumstances where projects with short (but very large) paybacks might be preferred – unless this impairs the portfolio balance.

Let us look at the following two opportunity streams of projects. Stream A consists of a one-off project with a good NPV but where cost is recouped slowly – in fact at the very end of the project. In Stream B there are a series of smaller projects with rapid pay-backs (and here a higher leverage of inflow relative to outlay).

	Stream A	Stream B		
		Project 1	Project 2	Project 3
Year 0	<10,000>	<1,000>		
Year 1				
Year 2		5,000	<1,000>	
Year 3				
Year 4			5,000	<1,000>
Year 5				
Year 6	30,000			5,000
Net present value (at 10%)	6,934	Net present value 3,132 (Total £7,858)	2,588	2,138

Stream A projects are typically capital investments, whereas Stream B projects are typically cost programmes. This illustration highlights the need to avoid not only being purely short-termist in thinking, but also *long-termist*. (Long-termist here is the mind-set of preferring longer-term projects over short-term projects of equivalent capacity to generate value.)

Strategy in action

illustration 7.4

A financial evaluation of activity-based management at ABC plc

Evaluating an investment in change management may be tricky, but it is by no means impossible. The route forward is to make some realistic assumptions about the project's share in benefits realised by the organisation at a wider level.

In ABC plc, a two-year programme to introduce an activity-based management system with direct costs of £200,000 per annum and £50,000 of indirect costs is being implemented. This might then lead on to a series of projects for managing cost more effectively in the business, with possible net savings of £500,000 in year 3, £800,000 in year 4, and £200,000 in year 5.

If we were to assume that 50 per cent of these benefits were due to this system (and 50 per cent to other changes, for example in the management culture), we see the following profile of costs:

Benefits £'000	Year 1	Year 2	Year 3	Year 4	Year 5
Project's share of savings 50%			250	400	100
Costs £'000					
Direct costs	200	200			
Indirect costs	50	50			
	250	250			
Net cash flows	(250)	(250)	250	400	100
Cumulative cash flows	(250)	(500)	(250)	150	250

This shows a payback occurring early in year 4. If we were to discount those net cash flows at 10 per cent this would give us (ignoring tax issues for simplicity and assuming cash flows occur at the end of each year):

	£'000	Discount Factor	Present Value £'000
Year 1	(250)	.91	(227)
Year 2	(250)	.83	(207)
Year 3	250	.75	187
Year 4	400	.68	272
Year 5	100	.62	62
		Net present value	87

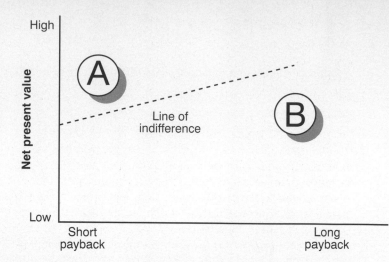

Note: this assumes that cash inflows from projects with short paybacks can be reinvested in further projects which beat the company's cost of capital.

Figure 7.6   *Trading off long- and short-term projects*

7.3.4   *Cost structure analysis*

Finally, before we leave financial management's contribution to strategic cost management, it is worthwhile just to touch on parts of cost theory which may seem to be self-evident but which are often neglected or misunderstood by managers. Here we need to understand the split between fixed and variable costs, and the trade-offs between having a mainly fixed versus variable cost base for instance BA's, 'Step Change' prunes back fixed costs – reducing British Airways' vulnerability to a cyclical market.

For example, if a company's cost base is £10 million and half of the costs are fixed, a quarter are 80 per cent fixed and the remainder are 90 per cent fixed, we have:

	£'000 Costs	£'000 Fixed	£'000 Variable
First	5,000	5,000	–
Next	2,500	2,000	500
Next	2,500	2,250	250
	10,000	9,250	750

In this case, variable costs are a mere 7.5 per cent of total costs, or on a turnover of, say, £12 million, just over six per cent.

Two key points of note here are:

- many costs are taken for granted, for example 'fixed' costs may be fixed short term but variable or part-variable longer term. (At British Airways it was possibly taken for granted before 'Step Change' that 'we had to do these things ourselves')

- there are often trade-offs between cost structure (fixed, variable and semi-variable costs) and the level of operational flexibility. (In the above example one might out-source £2 million of fixed costs. Assuming that no cost savings occur by switching the types of resource, this change would increase variable costs to 27.5 per cent of the cost base. By increasing the proportion of the cost base which is variable this *protects* the company in the event of a reduction in market demand. In British Airways' case, for example, it might be unwise to swap fixed costs for variable costs if the market expanded rapidly. Clearly, the preference for variable versus fixed costs is dependent on a market scenario – and the associated competitive conditions.

Financial management thus provides some useful inputs into strategic cost management through ABC, through appraising longer-term cost programmes as quasi-investment decisions and also through achieving a deeper understanding of cost structures.

7.4 *An operations management perspective on costs*

The main operations management themes of most relevance to strategic cost management are those of:

- quality
- customer service

7.4.1 *Quality management*

Turning first to quality, quality interfaces with cost management in three main ways. First, quality may add superior value to the external customer. By improving quality one might actually add more value to the customer than previously. But how will that value actually be harvested by the company? There are a number of ways in which this might occur:

- Through reducing the likelihood and frequency of switching to another supplier
- Through reducing the costs of preventing the customer from switching (for example, through reduced advertising and promotion and costs of customer visits).

It is rare for all of the higher prices gained through superior quality

Strategy in action

illustration 7.5

Evaluating customer acquisition costs

Evaluating the costs of acquiring new customers is typically made at an intuitive, gut-feel level. This example shows not only how these costs can be weighed and evaluated but also how this evaluation feeds into action.

A small consultancy firm had consulted with a major supermarket chain, 'Bestco' plc, for a number of years, working at Trading Director level. Its fees over the years 1994 to 1997 had been around £8,000 – £12,000 per annum, giving it a beach-head in the company but one which it sought to break out of.

Its Director had been interested in working at Board level for some time and was hoping to achieve this 'value migration' (see Chapter 2) when opportunities arose.

The chance to meet its new Chief Executive arose in 1997 but this required doing a day off-fees. Although this seemed a long shot and the loss of around, say, £1,000 of fee income (which was painful for a small firm), the opportunity to invest the time was taken.

Subjectively, this opportunity gave at best a 10 per cent chance of achieving this value breakthrough. But had this generated an incremental £5,000 a year of fees for the next five years (or £25,000) this would have yielded an 'expected value' (or the estimated probability of an event multiplied by its pay-off) of –10 x £25,000, or £2,500. (This ignores the spin-off effects of using this breakthrough to penetrate Board-level work at other plc's – or 'opportunity value' – see Chapter 5).

Clearly, the actual out-turn of value captured will be either zero, or of the order of £25,000. For the really determined manager who is dedicated to the 'hunt for value' this probability profile would not be enough – so how can the odds be improved?

untangle them. Instead, one should look at organisational change as involving a single, strategic cost programme which can only really be evaluated by:

- generating a 'base case' for organisational costs – what will the costs look like *without* major change – given incremental changes in organisational structure and extrapolating the existing style and culture. This begins to define the gap between the current cost base and the required future cost base (17)

- developing an organisational strategy. This involves looking at how the capability of the organisation can be developed to meet the external and competitive needs, and at what cost

- devising change programmes (for example, operational, people-related, or culture change) which might support the overall organisational strategy. (In BA's case this would involve putting in place support programmes to enable managers to be effective in the 'New World')

- appraising the cost outlay of organisational change relative to its illustrative benefits as a strategic investment decision

Organisational analysis requires evaluating change programmes which can apply value management too, as we will see next.

7.5.2   *How might strategic change be valued?*

Many managers may be aware of the need to *evaluate* strategic change (18). However, they may be less aware of the possibility of actually putting a (financial) value on strategic change, ie its *valuation*.

It may seem a most daunting task to value strategic change because of the difficulty of defining a) the key objectives of many change programmes, and b) the key organisational shifts which are necessary to achieve these objectives.

A five-stage approach may help simplify these hurdles:

- the objectives and key issues: the change objective may be set by applying a balanced-score-card approach to defining the key objectives of the change (19).
- the underlying shifts on 'how we do things around here' or the paradigm (20): 'From and To' analysis may be to diagnose the key organisational shifts necessary to underpin the change (see Table 7.1)
- valuing the change: value-based techniques may be applied to the cost/benefit analysis of the proposed change
- assessing the implementation difficulty: this difficulty might be evaluated by analysing the organisational forces impacting on implementation
- building a business case: a business case methodology may be applied to appraise the value of the change and to prioritise it against other change projects using an attractiveness/implementation difficulty grid.

We now elaborate briefly on these five stages.

First, a balanced score-card approach to the change helps it to be more effectively targeted in terms of identifying the:

- specific and tangible, financial benefits
- softer improvements in market and competitive position
- operational benefits (such as greater speed and flexibility) – tangible in nature but hard to quantify financially
- innovative capability in building new ideas which offer contingent value (14) – that is value which will only crystallise by alignment of a number of internal and external value drivers.

Table 7.1   *From and to analysis*

	From ⟶	To
Product range	*Complex*	*Simplified*
Culture	*Bureaucratic*	*Genuine Empowerment*
Processes	*Fragmented*	*Integrated*
Skills	*Variable quality*	*'World-class'*
Sourcing	*Mainly in-house*	*Strategic outsourcing*

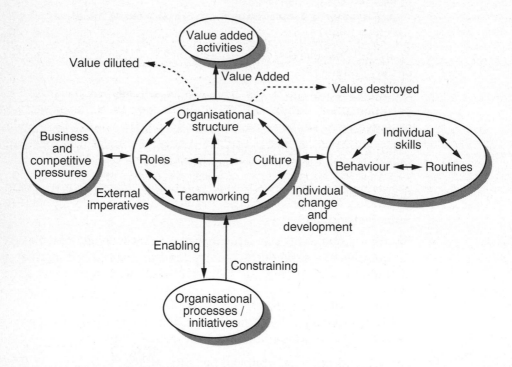

Figure 7.7   *Valuing strategic change*

Next, the key issues surrounding the strategic change can be mapped out by using the diagnostic in Figure 7.7. This helps us to avoid the trap of beginning with organisational structure – and ending up in an overly-charged political debate. Instead, organisational issues should be informed by an analysis of:

a) the business and competitive pressures impacting – now or in the future

b) the value added activities which are currently adding value, diluting value or destroying value (see, once again, Chapter 2 on 'Managing Strategy for Value').

Besides organisational structure, roles of key individuals (and how they work together) invariably need revisiting, as does the underlying culture. Besides individually focused changes there may also need to be new organisational processes or initiatives put in place. Equally, existing organisational processes/initiatives may need to be refocused or abandoned.

Figure 7.8 is particularly important owing to the frequency with which managers face the issue of changing organisational structure. These changes are of both personal and political sensitivity and hard to address objectively. Also, organisational structure itself is an important cost driver and therefore needs to be given special attention.

Second, 'From and to' (or 'FT') analysis can help identify the degree of underlying change necessary to support the specific change objective of a particular project. This also helps us to determine its acceptability (21). 'FT' analysis helps to identify the softer inter-dependencies which need to be aligned in order to reap the potential value of the change. 'FT' analysis will also help identify the key uncertainties and risks. Finally, 'FT' analysis can be of considerable

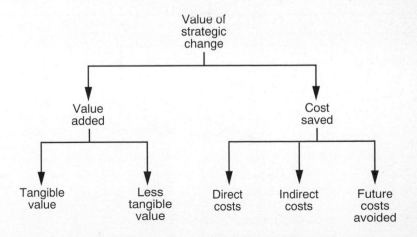

Figure 7.8   *Understanding value added versus costs saved of strategic change*

value in helping managers track the progress of strategic change – through a combination of financial, and non-financial indicators.

Third, in valuing the change, we need to consider a) targeting the benefits, and b) estimating the costs. Taking first a), Figure 7.9 illustrates the need to separate out incremental value added versus costs saved. Also less easily measurable benefits of speed and responsiveness need to be assessed.

Value added may need to be tested out to ensure that value added in theory (for example, via improved quality of service to customers) is harvested via incremental volumes or premium prices. This value is shared between customers and the company (see, again, Chapter 2).

Service times and responsiveness can also play an important role in contributing to value (22). Speed or responsiveness may create *possible* value (through, for instance, increased speed which might enable a company to service either more customers or more needs in the same time). Actually *harvesting* this value may, however, be interdependent with more effective marketing strategy or tactics.

Turning next to b) or cost estimation, costs of change might be either directly attributable to the change project or may be indirect (but within the same operation). There might also be knock-on costs, in other business units which need to be assessed. Looking only at the

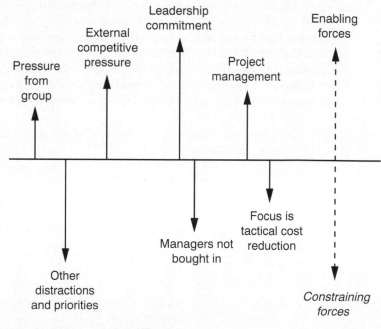

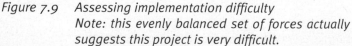

Figure 7.9   *Assessing implementation difficulty*
Note: this evenly balanced set of forces actually
suggests this project is very difficult.

direct and immediate costs of the programme and the direct benefits may provide a most misleading picture (positively or negatively) of the potential value of the change.

The fourth stage in the analysis is to assess the difficulty of the change using an approach derived from 'implementation forces' analysis.

Implementation forces analysis displays the key hard and soft forces which might enable or constrain effective implementation. See Figure 7.9 for an example of implementation forces analysis. The length of the arrows depicts the perceived strength of the force. Implementation forces analysis can be used both as a management tool *and* as a means of collecting data.

The importance of implementation constraints here for SFM is that these constraints:

- increase the cost of resources needed to achieve change
- slow down the implementation process – again increasing the costs
- frequently make the benefits fewer in number and more diluted – undermining value added.

7.6 *The strategic cost management process*

7.6.1 *The key phases of strategic cost management*

To implement strategic cost management effectively requires more than mere analytical skills – it also requires a process. For instance, at BA early warnings were heard about whether the company could bring on board the change needed to effect the new cost structure. Indeed *The Times* (6 November, 1996) went as far as to suggest that BA was pushing the speed and severity of change too far and too quickly and 'something will snap'.

This framework for a strategic cost management is based on the following premises:

- without a systematic process, costs are likely to be managed on a purely or predominantly tactical basis

- managing costs involves managers with many complex, cross-functional issues. These cross-functional issues need to be tackled therefore with a flexible set of tools. By using these tools within a team process this provides more challenge to the status quo and builds ownership of the change

- this suggests that an initial diagnosis phase is crucial. This involves identifying and prioritising issues prior to exploring and evaluating key options.

The process shown in Figure 7.10 illustrates therefore how costs can

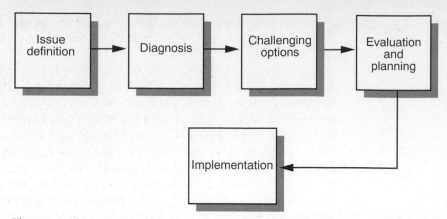

Figure 7.10   The strategic cost management process

be managed strategically – showing the stages of issue definition, diagnosis, challenging options, more detailed evaluation, planning and implementation. A process similar to this has been followed by Amersham International, by BP Chemicals and by Urenco (formerly part of British Nuclear Fuels) and the Bank of Ireland.

Following the diagnosis phase, the next stage is to create challenging options – this tests the status quo. This stage is separated from detailed planning and evaluation so that managers do not just reinvent the existing pattern of cost allocation in a naive way. This stage involves evaluating options using the attractiveness and implementation difficulty ('AID') grid tool (see below) to separate out:

- their inherent attractiveness (in cost/benefit terms). Ideally this boils down to quantitative and primarily financial indicators (these do not have to be exact). Initially this can be evaluated in a qualitative sense and later, perhaps, actually in hard, money terms
- the implementation difficulty – this requires assessing how hostile or receptive the organisation is to changing its allocation of resources to achieve project goals.

To illustrate how this prioritisation works, in Figure 7.11 we are able to compare a number of projects for cost improvement. Whilst project A appears to be of medium attractiveness and relatively easy to implement, project B looks equally attractive but is also much harder to implement. Project C offers much higher net benefit, still, but because of its apparent difficulty may be placed (erroneously) by management 'on the shelf'.

British Airways' 'Step Change', for example, would appear to be both 'Highly Attractive' and 'Very Difficult' (the latter being perhaps an understatement). But within this overall positioning on the AID grid (in the extreme North-East sector) individual projects could be appraised splitting out their different positions.

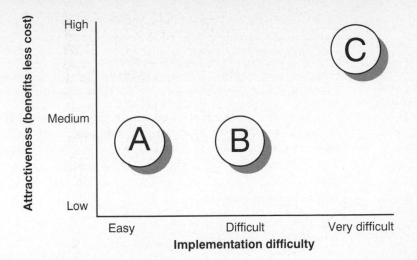

Figure 7.11   *Attractiveness and implementation difficulty ('AID') analysis (sometimes known as 'VD')*

The process can now be fleshed out using the checklists contained in the next section.

7.6.2   Issue definition

Before the diagnosis of issues it is necessary first of all to brainstorm all the possible areas which might be addressed before prioritising these for analysis.

Key questions to help identify the issues are:

1.   Which discretionary costs exist within the organisation that might be reduced?

2.   Which overhead costs are incurred which generate limited   value added to the customer (external or internal)?

3.   Are marketing, operations or financing costs being well targeted and monitored in relation to their value added? Should these be selectively increased on account of their value added? For example, Dyson (in Chapter 5) offered customers a new machine by courier in the event of breakdown – in order to underpin his premium price. (Industry commentators thought that he 'was mad' but he evidently wasn't.)

4.   Are cost information systems genuinely effective or do these suffer from poor quality inputs, outputs and dissemination?

5.   Is the prevailing culture a cost aware one? Is this one of overly frugal management or one which is relatively unconcerned with costs?

6. What 'sacred cows' exist which incur cost without adding significant value to the business and also set an inappropriate example for how costs are managed elsewhere?

7. Are the costs of the change process evaluated, targeted and then monitored and subject to a business case procedure?

The above checklist will probably give a number of possible issues to work on. During the next phase you need to take each issue separately and work these through the diagnosis checklists below.

At British Airways in 1997 the crucial issue was obviously highlighted by question 3 above on refocusing activities within the business value system.

7.6.3 Diagnosis of issues

1. How are costs made up and how can we creatively re-segment costs, for example by activity, channels, customer types, etc? (See, once again, the kinds of business segmentation techniques explored in Chapter 3, 'Strategic Management Accounting'.)

2. To what extent are costs recurring or non-recurring, and does this suggest clues as to how both of these areas of cost can be more effectively managed?

3. What are the key cost drivers both at macro level and also at a much more micro level? (See, again, the cost hierarchy approach – of supermarket trolleys, and the example in Figure 7.5.)

4. To what extent is poor quality or business complexity contributing to problems of controlling cost?

5. Which 20 per cent of areas of cost or cost drivers offers 80 per cent of the potential for improvement ('Pareto' analysis)? For example, which particular areas of cost are either a) managed loosely, or b) in a way remote from the market place, or c) are particularly large, either relative to the cost base or to the level of profit, or d) have not been challenged for some considerable time.

6. What is the gap between current cost levels and where you need to be (target cost levels)? (See our earlier Figure 7.4 on competitive cost targeting.)

7 How do these target costs stack up against the improvements .which competitors are likely to be able to make over that period?

8. What does an analysis of the unit costs of a particular unit of output suggest and how does this relate to the value of the output? (See Illustration 7.7 below.)

Strategy in action

illustration 7.6
Making comparisons of costs to net profit

Managers can find for themselves new ways of highlighting cost levels – to achieve the Surprise Effect.

A major European computer company decided to review the costs of its property portfolio. Because of difficulties of getting rid of certain property leases following a recession, these commitments had not been closely reviewed with a view to radical action. Also, these costs had been viewed as 'fixed' on each budget cycle, rather than as being potentially variable – and avoidable.

Although property-related costs were only approximately 8 per cent of the company's cost base, management's attention was drawn to the area when the company's management accountant pointed out the simple and obvious fact that property costs were over 160 per cent of operating profits.

Strategy in action

illustration 7.7
Unit cost analysis – what did a memo cost to send?

Managers can find for themselves new ways of highlighting cost levels – to achieve the Surprise Effect.

Unit cost analysis can provide management with some very big shocks which result in rapid action to counter value destruction.

A major accounting firm conducted a cost review of some of its administrative activities. (This was just before Electronic Mail became widely available.) Frequent memos were sent to all of its partners and senior managers in the South-East of England from policy matters down to invitations to staff leaving parties.

When the full costs of transmitting a memorandum to its 500 senior staff were assessed it transpired that the unit cost of a single memorandum was around £5,000 because of the costs of paper handling in the organisation.

As a result of the review only memoranda dealing with more strategic issues were despatched. Interestingly, at Dyson appliances memos are actually banned, - they are considered to be virtually value diluters or destroyers.

Having diagnosed one or more of your issues you are now able to create a number of challenging options for each one separately.

Clearly, BA has implicitly made use of question 4 (business complexity), question 5 (Pareto analysis), question 6 (gap analysis), and question 7 (competitor cost analysis).

For example, areas where British Airways almost certainly focused include question 1 (zero-based thinking) – to look at how its operations can be re-invented from scratch. It also appears to have considered question 2 (future cost base), particularly in thinking about future competitive conditions. It also no doubt has considered question 3 (cost benchmarking) particularly to reduce the costs of bought-in issues. It has also used question 5 (out-sourcing) where many of its traditionally 'core' activities are now seen as non-core. To some extent question 7 also applies (fixed cost substitution) and question 12 (restructuring the value system of not just the company but the industry).

7.6.4   *Creating challenging options*

1.   Can costs be challenged either by building up from a base of nothing, a 'zero-based approach', that is with no fixed assumptions of what is possible, or by building up from a low base of cost? (See Illustration 7.8 below for 'how to tackle' the zero-based approach.)

2.   Can target cost levels be established based on an assessment of how the business needs to compete effectively in, for example, one, three and even five years time?

3.   Have these targets for cost and quality been bench-marked externally to help target them competitively? This might involve, for example, visiting other companies outside your own industry – with a very clear agenda – to explore how they do things differently and better relative to your own organisation, and industry.

4.   Has management unfrozen existing thinking about costs by encouraging a 'Robbing Peter to Pay Paul' climate, thus investing resources released in areas which can add more value?

5.   Can costs be managed more effectively by substituting (in whole or in part) external for internal resource, thus refocusing the 'business activities that we are in'? (See Illustration 7.9 below, on Hewlett Packard.)

6.   Is capacity there on a 'just-in-case' basis and therefore being considerably under-utilised?

7.   Are areas of 'fixed cost' really all that fixed – especially in the long run? What trade-offs exist within the cost structure between fixed and variable costs – financially, operationally and competitively?

8.   What costs are based on internal allocations and transfer prices and are these justifiable on any economic basis?

Strategy in action

illustration 7.8
Zero-based thinking at ICL

Zero-based thinking is a creative approach to cost which begins by imagining, in effect, 'If there were a nuclear attack and we had to build again from scratch, what would we put in place?' Sometimes this means putting the same resources back – but working to a much simplified agenda.

An example of a zero-based approach was ICL Logistics review of its cost base (7). Before the 1990s ICL had mainly shipped large, expensive shipments of computer equipment. At that time the distribution costs were not a very high percentage of total costs, and thus were not so critical to the business.

By the early 1990s many of the shipments were of personal computers (PC's), with a smaller value per shipment. By this time the PC market had become much more competitive. As a result, ICL decided to conduct a review in which its line managers and supervisors addressed the following question:

'What would we bid to run this business for ICL if it were a management buy-out, assuming a "no-frills operation"?'

About 20 staff (at middle management and supervisory level) worked on this question for nearly three hours, coming back with the answer:

'About half of the current cost base.'

Interestingly, during the exercise the various sub-teams were torn in two directions – firstly to 'win the business' and secondly to 'reinvent old and more complex nice-to-have processes'. Eventually, their focus on competitive pressures generated new ways of re-designing the business value system to deliver equivalent value (to that added currently) but at a radically reduced level of cost.

9. Are there many less tangible areas of benefit attributed to cost programmes which currently are unchallenged and loosely targeted?

10. Are there areas where new investment could generate a rapid payback through cost reduction, but which have simply not been considered because of the internal financial climate?

11. Are there areas of business which we should simply get out of because external shifts in the environment have increased the cost base substantially?

12. Can the industry's or company's value system be restructured so as to give the company (sustainable) cost advantage?

Illustration 7.9 overleaf highlights again the need to address cost and value issues simultaneously. But it also underlines the

The above checklist should flush out the practical issues that need to be attended to in order to release the value of strategic cost management. These issues need painstaking management, not merely over months but frequently over one, two or even three years.

7.6.6   Implementation

Implementation is a most critical phase and invites some obvious and less obvious questions:

1. Has the project manager for the programme got the necessary time, the technical and interpersonal skills, business awareness and clout to manage this project effectively?

2. Have the key constraining forces been dealt with in the implementation plan?

3. In particular, does the implementation plan recognise the softer areas of change which also need to be managed effectively – particularly communication, feedback and motivation?

7.7   Conclusion

By now the argument for managing costs strategically through SCM is both overpowering and, we hope, complete. We have shown how costs can be managed as a coherent process – for both financial and competitive advantage. Strategic cost management is a vital tool in seeking breakthrough strategies for growth which genuinely add value. The SCM process draws in a variety of analysis tools and recipes for diagnosing cost issues, for creating challenging options and for testing implementation plans. It combines both qualitative and quantitative analysis to refocus both cost and value drivers.

Costs have often been relegated within finance as a 'systems' or budgetary issue. To a large extent they have been viewed as being merely operational and tactical. But they can actually play a major role either in enabling or frustrating strategies for growth.

But the increasingly competitive pressure we have seen over the past few years has put the spotlight very much on costs. This increase in competitive pressures has been accompanied by stagnant economic conditions, deregulation in many sectors and also many formerly growth industries reaching maturity. Sometimes this spotlight has been focused purely internally, and in the short term was without regard for the interdependencies within the business system. More rarely has cost management been sensitised to avoid the negative impact on competitive position. A way forward here is to highlight and amplify the message that this generates weaker financial performance

– not only longer term but also indirectly through impact in other functional areas.

Strategic cost management is therefore not merely a philosophy which integrates perspectives from strategic management, financial management, operations and organisational behaviour. It is also a practical approach which enables managers to rise up above the narrow and political budget games which hold back strategic development from achieving its full potential.

References

(1) See *Exploring Corporate Strategy*, Section 4.3.2
(2) See *Exploring Corporate Strategy*, Section 6.3
(3) Shank and Govindarajan, *Strategic Cost Management*, The Free Press, Macmillan, 1993
(4) Porter E. M., *Competitive Advantage*, The Free Press, Macmillan, 1985
(5) See *Exploring Corporate Strategy*, Section 6.3.1 which gives a more extensive coverage of cost leadership
(6) It is helpful here to apply the 'Strategy Clock' explained in *Exploring Corporate Strategy*, which illustrates further positionings such as 4b and 5 – for those readers familiar with *Exploring Corporate Strategy*, – see Section 6.3
(7) Grundy A. N., *Implementing Strategic Change*, Kogan Page, 1993
(8) The value chain is covered at length in *Exploring Corporate Strategy*, Section 4.3.1
(9) Kaplan R. S. and Johnson H. T., *Relevance Lost – The Rise and Fall of Management Accounting*, Harvard Business School Press, 1987
(10) Cooper R. and Kaplan R. S., *Profit Priorities from Activity based Costing*, Harvard Business Review, May-June, 1991
(11) Hammer M. and Champy J., *Re-engineering the Corporation*, Nicholas Brealey Publishing, London, 1993
(12) Hammer M. and Stanton A., *The Re-engineering Revolution*, Hammer & Co, 1995
(13) Tomkins C, *Corporate Resource Allocation – Financial, Strategic and Organisational Perspectives*, Basil Blackwell, 1991
(14) Grundy A N, *Breakthrough Strategies for Growth*, Pitman, 1995
(15) See *Exploring Corporate Strategy*, Section 6.3
(16) See *Exploring Corporate Strategy*, Chapters 9, 10 and 11
(17) This requires a 'gap analysis' – see *Exploring Corporate Strategy*, Section 8.2.2
(18) See *Exploring Corporate Strategy*, Section 11.3 which describes how to diagnose change needs
(19) See *Exploring Corporate Strategy*, Section 10.4.3

(20)   See *Exploring Corporate Strategy*, Section 2.4.1

(21)   See *Exploring Corporate Strategy*, Section 8.3

(22)   Stalk E., *Competing Against Time*, The Free Press, 1990

Part 4
Implementing strategic financial management

In our final chapter on review and conclusions we summarise the key messages of this book, particularly for implementation. We then draw out the many lessons on implementing strategic financial management from the (disguised) case study on TDC plc, a large, international company.

This case study highlights the need to think very carefully about the cultural implications of using SFM to change planning and control processes. It also underlines the need to manage key stakeholders proactively throughout implementation.

8 Review and conclusions

8.1 Introduction

In this chapter we will first summarise the contribution of strategic financial management (SFM) to good strategic management. We then encapsulate some of the key ideas of SFM in a series of diagnostic questions. These questions can then be applied both to practical business situations and to analysing case studies. We then consider some of the key issues of implementing SFM in our case study of TDC plc.

8.2 Strategic financial management – a summary

Strategic management is a process involving strategic analysis, choice and implementation. Therefore it is concerned with the deployment and re-deployment of resources to achieve a superior return (relative to competitors) (1).

Whilst strategic management is a most creative, fluid (and frequently *qualitative*) discipline, it should be equally concerned with value creation. Even when strategy analysts discuss the external positioning of a business, they should also have in mind the hoped-for cash streams which accrue from a strong competitive position. Any strategic *vision* must be accompanied by the understanding of how it will generate financial value. One of the key lessons from SFM is that you don't have to quantify everything (financially) to be thinking about value creation.

This means that strategic decision-making should not be dominated *either* by the urge to go in a particular strategic direction or by the overriding need to meet a preconceived financial return.

To bridge the gap between strategy and value we therefore need to:

- understand the workings of the business value system (see Chapter 2)

- manage value and cost drivers more explicitly and proactively (see Chapter 2)

- use strategic management accounting to help us identify the underlying drivers of performance much more effectively (see Chapter 3).

- apply strategic financial accounting in diagnosing the strategic (and financial) position, business performance and potential fit together by using published financial reports as source data (see Chapter 4).

In Chapters 5-7 we then examined a number of areas for applying SFM, including investment decisions, acquisitions and strategic cost management.

Investment decisions are often considered to be more concerned with corporate finance and the financial appraisal of projects than they are with strategic management. But many of the complexities of investment appraisal (for instance, uncertainty, intangibles and interdependencies) become understandable when strategic and financial appraisal are looked at as an integrated process.

Acquisitions provide an additional set of challenges. Here, we saw the need to control over-enthusiasm for ill-thought through corporate expansion through acquisition. This occurs when the strategic, organisational and financial implications of an acquisition are not well thought through. Further, the value added, diluted or destroyed by an acquisition needs to be explored by understanding the inherent value of the strategy (V1), the deal value (V2), and the integration value (V3).

Strategic cost management helped us to focus on internal resource allocation – ensuring that costs were managed for *both* financial *and* competitive advantage. Cost levels play a key role in determining the capacity of a company (like, for instance, British Airways) to meet external, competitive pressure. The level of a company's costs needs to be managed not merely short term but also to achieve longer-term targets. These targets need to reflect not only where key competitors' cost levels are currently, but also where they will be in the future.

Strategic financial management has thus demonstrated its role as an essential part of the strategic management toolkit. It helps both general and financial managers to expand their thinking when 'doing the numbers' so that they also:

- work on the right numbers in the first place (for instance, moving from a 'profit' focus to a 'cash flow' focus, and from the short term to the medium/longer term)

- use more appropriate data inputs (moving from localised performance measures to a broader understanding of the business value system, and from internal data only, to using a good mix of both external and internal data)

- present financial numbers in more meaningful ways (for example, by first segmenting 'the business we are in' and by using 'fishbone' (root cause) analysis and performance driver analysis) (see Chapter 3)

- apply SFM not merely to *evaluate* the present strategy, but also to create new strategic options, which will in the longer term add incremental shareholder value.

According to our 'AID' grid (Chapter 7), SFM is thus an *attractive* process to apply in order to generate value from corporate and business strategy. Managers need to recognise, however, that there are likely to be significant implementation difficulties, particularly in overcoming cultural barriers to change in the management process.

SFM is therefore not something merely for the Finance Department to own, but it must be championed by the Chief Executive, by the Board, and executed by all the senior line managers.

In this chapter we include a short case study on a 'Top 10' plc company which addresses some of the key implementation pitfalls facing SFM. This stresses:

- the need to position SFM not as yet another initiative but as 'the way we will manage strategy for value' – and as a permanent process

- the imperative of getting ownership for, and real commitment to, SFM at Chief Executive and Board level

- the need to manage SFM at a Group level, and not merely to introduce it within a division

- the inevitability of line managers finding it hard to reconcile (at least initially) old and new measures, imperatives and behaviours

- the benefit of getting real, tangible value out of the business portfolio as a result of SFM *within the first 18 months to two years*.

SFM, in summary, should not be seen as an 'easy-to-do, easy to harvest' set of techniques, but as a process which reaps considerable rewards. But if, and only if, managers are persistent.

8.3 *Checklists for strategic financial management*

In this section we now provide some high-level checklists for strategic financial management. These checklists are structured according to Chapters 2–10 as follows:

- Managing for value
- Strategic management accounting
- Strategic financial accounting
- Strategic investment decisions
- Acquisitions
- Strategic cost management

8.3.1   Managing for value

1. What are the main activities which generate value?

2. How do these interact as the 'business value system', and how is this system likely to change over time either due to external or internal change, or both?

3. What are the key value and cost drivers, and how could these be managed more effectively?

8.3.2   Strategic management accounting

1. How have we defined our strategic business units (SBUs) and is this appropriate?

2. What is their relative performance, and why is it that some are performing better than others (examining the key performance drivers)?

3. How do life-cycle effects impinge on performance, and how should these be managed?

4. What is the break-even point of each business area; can it be reduced and, if so, how?

8.3.3   Strategic financial accounting

1. What is the strategic intent of the company (given statements made in the Annual Report, and reading between the lines)?

2. What are the trends in past financial performance, and what patterns emerge?

3. How do these past trends appear to be influenced by changing competitive and organisational conditions?

4. What do the various financial ratios tell us, particularly about:
    • areas for breakthrough and continuous improvement
    • bottlenecks which need attention
    • weaknesses in our competitive strategy?

5. Where in the businesses is shareholder value being created, diluted or destroyed?

8.3.4   Strategic investment decisions

1. What is the scope of the investment project, and how does it link to other areas of investment?

2. What are its specific strategic objectives and what role do they play in the business value system?

3. What are the likely cash flows (of the business) with a 'do-nothing' scenario (the base case)?

4. What are the main value (and cost) drivers which will determine incremental cash flows?

5. What are the critical interdependencies of the project?

6. What are the key uncertainties and which of these are most important?

7. Are there any intangibles, and how (ultimately) will these generate value?

8. What is the appropriate cost of capital?

9. Can the project be reshaped to increase the NPV and/or shorten the payback?

8.3.5   Acquisitions

1. What are the strategic objectives of the acquisition?

2. How does the target fit the acquisition criteria (and what are these criteria and are they sufficiently specific to weed out targets which will not create value)?

3. What type of value will the acquisition create, particularly:
   • opportunity creation
   • synergistic
   • protective
   • 'sweat' value?

4. How will this value be manifest, particularly in terms of:
   • V1 = the coherent value of the strategy
   • V2 = the value created or destroyed during the deal
   • V3 = the value created, diluted or destroyed during integration/post-acquisition management?

5. What are the key uncertainties surrounding the acquisition and how can these be managed?

6. What is the total investment required to make the purchase and to integrate and develop the acquisition (the 'iceberg' model of investment)?

7. What other options are available, other than a straight acquisition, for example:
   • an alliance (or joint venture)
   • organic development?

8.3.6 Strategic cost management

1. How does the current allocation of resources match the competitive positioning of the businesses?

2. What should (or could) our target cost base look like (bearing in mind too where our competitors' cost bases are heading)?

3. What would this enable us to do (that we cannot do currently)?

4. What are the key cost drivers and how could we manage these more effectively?

5. How could we simplify the business to reduce our costs, and/or add more value?

6. How could we build up costs from a zero or low base – to add more value?

7. If we were able to spend more than our current perceived constraint, where would we get most value?

Case study 8.1

Strategic financial management at 'The Drink Company International'

8.1.1 Introduction

Strategic financial management is a philosophy rather than a quick fix. Introducing it to an organisation requires sensitivity to the organisational culture and controls, and to its key stakeholders – and their perceptions, their power base and fears. The TDC case study shows not only that implementing strategic financial management can be highly attractive, it can also be relatively difficult – unless these factors are thoroughly understood.

8.1.2 Implementing SFM at TDC plc

TDC is a major international subsidiary of a top 10 plc; it is global in focus with a UK head office. Its portfolio includes large number consumer brands marketed and sold on a worldwide basis.

This case illustration brings out the many practical issues, which need to be dealt with in implementing SFM.

In the early 1990s, two senior TDC managers participated in action research into strategic financial management at Cranfield School of Management. At that time there was some interest at TDC in using shareholder value techniques to evaluate business strategies. However, the organisational conditions at that time were probably not ripe within TDC for applying the philosophy of managing for value to the point where it could gain a critical mass.

Richard Black (who was then Finance Director for TDC Europe) participated in this early review. In 1990 he expressed concerns about reconciling:

a) an *economic value-based* approach to evaluating major organic and acquisitive decisions (using discounted cash flow), and with

b) TDC's business and financial targets and controls, which were based on shorter-term profitability measures.

Richard Black's interest in managing for value had therefore been awakened. This awakening primed him to become a catalyst in TDC's migration from traditional financial measures to value-based management between 1994 and 1996. During this time he was TDC's Director of Corporate Development.

This short case study highlights the problems of managing SFM at a practical level, and especially in how it makes the transition from old to new ways of doing things. In effect, TDC was trying to change its controls, its routines and its management rituals (see the 'culture web' of *Exploring Corporate Strategy*, Figure 2.10) to create a paradigm shift in its management style. It also impacted on its power structures. In our final section of the case study we look at some of the key implementation issues which SFM faced at TDC. This applies both to the 'culture web' and an adapted version of stakeholder analysis (see *Exploring Corporate Strategy*). The process which TDC went through can be summarised (at a macro level) in Figure 8.1.

The SFM process began with the perception that a value gap existed between currently projected value creation and corporate and divisional financial targets. These targets reflected shareholder aspirations. TDC then performed a review of business areas. This review established the extent to which these businesses currently created, diluted or destroyed value. It also examined their potential to create value in the future.

This phase led to a more detailed examination of increasing investment or decreasing investment options. A particular issue was the need to reduce product complexity – in particular parts of worldwide distribution. In addition, TDC needed to consider the country/market priorities and strategic options associated with these.

In parallel, the corporate and divisional financial targets influenced tactical objectives, which in turn fed into thinking within business plans (along with views on longer-term investment/divestment). But equally important were the external pressures facing the managers of business units.

Case study 8.1

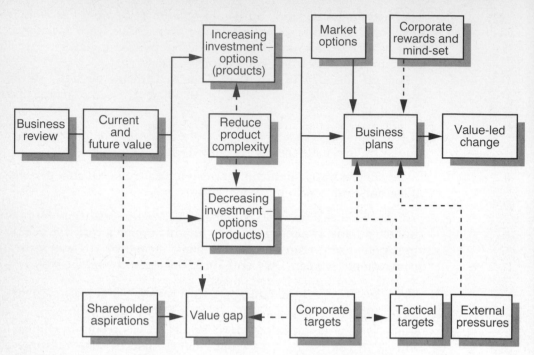

Figure 8.1   Strategic financial management – at TDC International

Besides these internal and external influences on business plans, corporate rewards and mind-set also had a pervasive role. As we will see it took some time before these softer factors began to realign and facilitate value-led change in both operations and management. In the following section our own commentary is italicised.

8.1.3   SFM at TDC – key implementation themes

The key implementation themes in the TDC case are:

- increasing investment
- reducing investment
- dealing with product complexity
- country participation
- SFM as culture change.

Increasing investment

Richard Black explained some of the benefits of the process, particularly when reviewing extra product investment.

'We did a lot of work on a major product in the USA, with the marketeers playing a central role to evaluate the effects of changing our advertising spend to secure more shareholder value.'

'This change in strategy is working well. Because we put in extra advertising we were able to increase the price. We are seeing quite significant improvements in performance.'

'This investment had been pretty successful both financially and in building Brand Equity. People felt that it showed we were committed over time, and that they would be protected. Although in certain circumstances, because of the focus on getting year-end figures, we have actually cut expenditure which created a credibility issue.'

'The managers said: "You mean you still expect us to deliver all your longer-term financial targets. But you reduce our current investment simply to achieve our short-term financial targets." '

Expectations about what SFM will lead to in the way of resource reallocation thus play an important role in determining whether it will be incorporated as a management process or rejected with cynicism.

Reducing investment

Besides highlighting products to increase investment, SFM may also identify products to reduce investment.

'People often believe that if we find a negative economic profit (in a particular business area) then this inevitably means an exit strategy.'

'For instance, one particular product was a value destroyer. But what you may have noticed is that it hasn't been on the television for the past two years. We couldn't justify the advertising investment that we were incurring on television to stimulate extra volume and margin. So we have taken that spend away. This has helped to move profitability in the direction of value creation even though it still consumes value and ironically volume has not significantly declined.'

In conclusion, although a product may destroy value, there may still be options for retaining it, for example by reducing the level of ongoing investment.

Dealing with product complexity

SFM can play a major role in re-engineering and simplifying the business strategy. Richard Black continues:

'We are far more ruthless now with new brand development. We are cutting out things which fail. We may say, yes, we can tolerate that brand for the next three years destroying value, but you do recognise that it is this much this year, and it is this much next year, and after that we expect it to come through and add positive value.'

The goal of simplification becomes more difficult because of problems with justifying reduced profit contribution.

'But the real difficulty is to say "what is the incremental effect, for example of just taking one brand out?" Our view might be that we can sell a brand for a certain amount of money, but everybody else then says "what about the rest of the portfolio, it doesn't do anything for us". But actually it does, it clutters up the system, all of your stock, our stock turnover ratios, it does all of those things and there is no simple way of analysing the cost.'

'For example, we have a sales force that sells three major products (and many minor ones). If we reduce our range of brands we have to consider what do we do with the overheads that are left over.'

He then takes a step back from this to reflect on the bigger implications for the brand portfolio.

'It is also linked to the question of size of brand portfolio. We have got so many brands – we have a lot of secondary brands now – it is cluttering the portfolio. But there is a reluctance to take them out because they are generating contribution.'

'If you take all the major products in our portfolio, and if you look at a certain product, without question it would improve the quality of the portfolio, but would it really mean that you would get extra margin?'

So, in conclusion, simplifying the product portfolio is frequently an essential – although tricky – part of beginning to bridge the gap between destroying value and beginning to add value (or the 'value gap').

Country participation

In addition to product-based decisions, TDC also has to understand country participation issues. Richard Black explores this as follows:

'With one non-core product where we weren't putting in any investment at all but which was important in some countries, we found it was destroying a lot of shareholder value.'

'But we found a local company who required additional capacity, so they got benefits out of it. We were then able to keep the distribution in the two key markets which we wanted, and we only lost a small amount of contribution. We got rid of all the assets, all the problems of manufacture, and we retained our distribution where we wanted it, and sub-contracted production of two other brands at reduced costs. So that was a great deal – there were benefits to us and there were benefits to them. This was really a two plus two equals five.'

'In one country we have reduced our overheads whilst retaining our market position. In another country we have said we are not going to be here on the ground but we are going to give our brands to a distributor. So we have proactively reduced value destruction without jeopardising our brand's market position.'

Obviously, where a company has a matrix of product and country markets, this adds an additional dimension to SFM. Here we need to look at both the implications of options across markets (for a product) and options across products (for a particular country market).

SFM as culture change

Richard Black recognised that linking strategy and value inevitably meant a major change in management culture – and it was therefore not just a project with a particular end point.

'One of the major difficulties that we had was the perception that this was a project, and that it is not a fundamental behaviour change. TDC is great at central initiatives where you go away and you persuade people that something new is important. And because of that decision people saw the process as a one-off.'

SFM had a considerable impact over both local and group level power structures:

'The big lesson, if we wanted to do it more quickly, was that the holding company had to buy in. We weren't managing the interface which said "earnings" were more important than value – and that was a big, big lesson.'

In summary, the corporate culture is thus a major factor which will facilitate or constrain the application of SFM. It can take considerable time and persistence to achieve sufficient change in understanding and behaviour to bring about value-led change.

'Prior to SFM, people's objectives were market share and that maximised operating profit – that's not value creation. For example, when making an acquisition, previously managers in businesses around TDC would have signed a bit of paper about how much of the new brands acquired they would sell. But when you go back to them post-acquisition and say "Hey, how are the brands doing?" they would say "Well, you know, I am being told to concentrate on my core brands, therefore this brand is deprived of financial and people resource".'

In conclusion, linking strategy and value (through SFM) is part of a particular management culture rather than being simply a bundling of analytical management techniques that give us a 'better answer'.

8.1.4   Lessons from TDC International

Despite these problems, TDC management have made some major breakthroughs in managing shareholder value employing the SFM philosophy. This has been achieved despite the complexity of dealing with a number of implementation themes of increasing investment, decreasing investment, dealing with product complexity and country participation.

The lessons from this process (as from earlier documented cases such as at BP, where it took almost five years to achieve the full benefits (2)) are that SFM needs the complete and sustained backing of corporate management from the top down in order to be successful. SFM, if implemented partially and without deep commitment, will only deliver limited benefits.

But SFM is one of the essential ways of making strategic management a reality – particularly in stretching managers' vision from the short term. And after three years it is being adopted by TDC as the key process in managing the organisation. The full benefits of SFM at TDC would not have been realised had SFM been considered merely an overhaul of 'how we do the plans and our numbers around here'. Real strategic decisions at the corporate and business level and a change in management mind-set need to occur for 'Managing for Value' to realise *its full value.*

8.1.5   Reflections on SFM as a change process

The TDC case study highlights the importance of anticipating and managing implementation issues in applying SFM. Using the culture web analysis from *Exploring Corporate Strategy*, we see very rapidly how significant SFM is in changing the management paradigm. Figure 8.2 highlights the many issues which are raised for SFM, requiring considerable management attention and stamina to surmount.

Figure 8.2 shows the importance of power and organisational structures in determining how the business is run, and how key decisions are taken, particularly in resource allocation. It also highlights how the basis of control changes with SFM (from

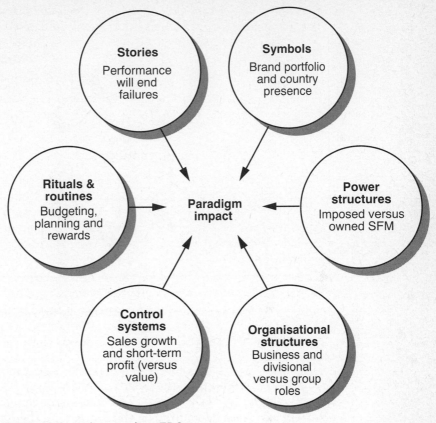

Figure 8.2   *SFM and the culture web at TDC*

sales/growth and short-term profits orientated to economic value added).

Rituals and routines all have a role to play both in the planning processes, through budgeting, planning and in the rewards systems. Stories and symbols provide the softer, cultural elements which can be found in the themes of conferences, in stories of performance crisis or failures (on what basis is success ascribed?) and in the meaning created by having certain brands and being in certain countries.

This all implies that SFM represents a major culture change programme. To implement SFM in a large organisation can take a number of years, as BP found, for example, between 1988 and 1992 (2).

Besides the culture web, the positions of stakeholders play a powerful role in facilitating or constraining SFM. Figure 8.3 now plots the approximate positions of stakeholders in terms of attitude and also influence (over *both* the decision to implement SFM *and* over its effective implementation).

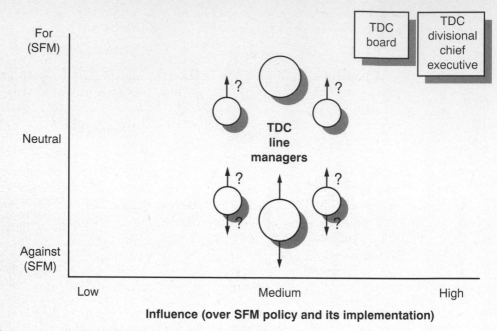

Figure 8.3　*SFM and key stakeholders – at TDC*

Figure 8.3 highlights the positive attitude of both TDC's Chief Executives and the TDC Board. TDC line managers are positioned in a variety of places, depending on the context, on their perceptions, and on their mix of agendas (and concerns). Figure 8.3 thus suggests that a considerable amount of effort is needed to win over managers who are hovering on the neutral line.

Our analysis of some of the key drivers of implementation difficulty suggests very strongly that SFM would be relatively difficult to implement at TDC, but also is very attractive (in terms of overall benefits less costs).

8.4　*Final conclusion*

Strategic financial management is a process which integrates a diversity of techniques. These techniques cover value analysis generally, and processes to deal with specific issues such as strategic investment decisions and cost management (internally) and acquisitions (externally) – see again Chapter 1. SFM gives managers considerable flexibility in dealing with strategic and financial issues faced by businesses beyond the 1990s and into the 21st century.

Virtually every major company's annual report and accounts today espouses the need to manage for *shareholder value* and is dotted with references to 'strategy'. But whilst managers may see the imperatives of strategic financial management, they may well feel less confident about *how* to implement it. The TDC case study highlights that these issues must be faced up to.

A hopeful sign of progress is the growing interest by both general managers and financial managers in the links between strategy and finance which is the concern of SFM. Conferences on value management appear to be brimming with managers – who are undeterred by their not insignificant cost.

Besides helping resolve theories and dilemmas over which SBUs to grow, harvest or dilute, SFM may also finally alleviate one of the most important stumbling blocks to strategic management – financial short-termism. Eventually, even the strategy and financial 'monsters' that we began with in Chapter 1 may come to the consensus that 'we are seeing and saying the same things' – and feel we want to behave the same way.

References

(1)   See *Exploring Corporate Strategy*, Chapter 1
(2)   Grundy A. N., *Corporate Strategy and Financial Decisions*, Kogan Page, 1992

References

Brealey R. and Myers S., *Principles of Corporate Finance*, McGraw Hill, 1984

Cooper R. and Kaplan R. S., *Profit Priorities from Activity-based Costing*, Harvard Business Review, May–June, 1991

Copeland T., Koller T., Murrin J., *Valuation – Measuring and Managing the Value of Companies*, J Wiley, 1990

Ellis J. and Williams D., *Corporate Strategy and Financial Analysis*, Pitman Publishing, 1993

Ghemawat P., *Commitment – The Dynamic of Strategy*, The Free Press, Macmillan, New York, 1991

Grundy A. N., *Breakthrough Strategies for Growth*, Pitman, 1995

Grundy A. N., *Corporate Strategy and Financial Decisions*, Kogan Page, 1992

Grundy A. N., *Implementing Strategic Change*, Kogan Page, 1993

Grundy A. N. and Ward K., (eds) *Strategic Business Finance*, Kogan Page, 1996

Hammer M. and Champy J., *Re-engineering the Corporation*, Nicholas Brealey Publishing, London, 1993

Hammer M. and Stanton A., *The Re-engineering Revolution*, Hammer & Co, 1995

Hertzberg F., *The Motivation to Work*, John Wiley and Sons, New York, 1959

Jemison D. B. and Sitkin S. B., *Acquisitions: The Process can be a Problem*, pp 107–116, Harvard Business Review, Boston, March – April 1996

Kaplan R. S. and Johnson H. T., *Relevance Lost – The Rise and Fall of Management Accounting*, Harvard Business School Press, 1987

Lewin K., *A Dynamic Theory of Personality*, McGraw Book Company, New York, 1935

Mitroff I. I. and Linstone H. A., *The Unbounded Mind*, Oxford University Press, 1993

Porter E. M., *Competitive Advantage*, The Free Press, Macmillan, 1985

Rappaport A., *Creating Shareholder Value*, The Free Press, New York, 1986

Reimann B., *Managing for Value: A Guide to Value-Based Strategic Management*, Basil Blackwell, Oxford, 1990

Shank J. K. and Govindarajan V., *Strategic Cost Management*, Free Press, Macmillan, 1993

Slywotzky J., *Value Migration*, Harvard Business School Press, 1996

Stalk E., *Competing Against Time*, The Free Press, 1990

Stewart G. B., *The Quest for Value*, Harperbusiness, 1991

Tomkins C., *Corporate Resource Allocation – Financial, Strategic and Organisational Perspectives*, Basil Blackwell, 1991

Waldrop M. M., *Complexity*, Penguin Books, 1992

Ward K., *Corporate Financial Strategy*, Butterworth Heinemann, 1993

Index